SCORNED, TORN
AND REBORN

SCORNED, TORN AND REBORN

Ending a Marriage with Integrity and Expanding into Your Better, Happier Life

REBECCA DONOVAN

LIFESTYLE
ENTREPRENEURS
PRESS
LAS VEGAS, NV

ISBN: 978-1-948787-05-5

Published by
Lifestyle Entrepreneurs Press
Las Vegas, NV

If you are interested in publishing through Lifestyle Entrepreneurs Press, write to:
Publishing@LifestyleEntrepreneursPress.com

To learn more about our publications or about foreign rights acquisitions of our catalogue books, please visit: www.LifestyleEntrepreneursPress.com

Printed in the USA

Acknowledgement

I would like to take this opportunity to give heartfelt thanks to my wonderful friends, Nilda, Keely, Cathe, and Teresa. They were there for me when I needed them most. They listened to me, consoled me, and encouraged me, no matter how many times I called. I especially want to thank Nilda and Keely for reading the first version of this book. I knew they would be both honest and kind, and they did not disappoint.

I also want to thank Jesse, Kristen, Zora, and Maira of Lifestyle Entrepreneurs Press, for the handholding and encouragement to complete this project.

Scorned, Torn and Reborn

Ending a Marriage with Integrity and Expanding into Your Better, Happier Life

SCORNED, TORN AND REBORN

Introduction

Start Here

He wants out. Now what?

You thought marriage was forever. Sure, there were ups and downs. Every marriage has them. But you thought the vows, the commitment, the love, and maybe just the sheer tenacity would prevail and keep the marriage afloat. We all wanted to believe in the fairy tale that love could (and would) conquer all. You can love someone—genuinely, faithfully, unconditionally love someone—and they can feel the same about you. Unfortunately, that doesn't always mean the two of you can be happily married to each other. Love **CANNOT** conquer all. There are many other factors that have to be present in order for a marriage to succeed. These factors include, but are not limited to, admiration, respect, compassion, compatibility, sexual compatibility, compromise, trust, and commitment. Perhaps you had all of those and still something was missing. Now your husband has pulled the rug out from under you, and your whole world is crashing down around you. You can't sleep. You can't eat. Half the time, you can't even think, except to ask, "Why?"

In this book we do explore the why. We have to before we can get to the real question: What now? You have a choice to make. Do you want this breakup to define you? Do you want to crawl to your corner and say that this was as good as it's ever going to get? Do you blame your husband for every problem in your marriage and now want to get revenge at any cost? Do you want to become bitter and sad and lonely forever? If you answered yes to any of those questions, then this book is *not* for you. We are not here to assign blame or make excuses or get even. We are here to help get you through this difficult process with your head held high, your dignity intact, and your integrity leading the way front and center. In reading this book, you will explore what was missing in your marriage and what you need to do for yourself to fill those gaps. You will find the means necessary for taking care of yourself—mind, body, and spirit. You will do exercises that encourage you to move forward with your new life. Along the way there is practical advice for the financial and legal process, co-parenting, as well as guidelines for discovering and creating the new you. You are going to come out on the other side of this would-be tragedy whole. You have an opportunity here to explore what you want and where you want to be. Discover who you want to be. There is no longer anyone standing in your path, blocking the way to your personal growth, enlightenment, and achievement. This is your chance to be reborn.

I have divided the book into three distinct sections. The first part of the journey is when you are reeling from shock, grief, betrayal—feeling **Scorned**. The second part is during the divorce process. You may be feeling angry, confused, and overwhelmed—feeling **Torn**. The last section is all about moving forward with your life to become the person you want to be, the new, improved you—**Reborn**.

Throughout the book I give advice and recommendations based on personal experience, the experiences of people I know, invaluable hindsight, and, of course, the benefit of hundreds of hours of reading. Each chapter is divided into subtopics, which you can easily and quickly refer back to as you navigate specific aspects of the divorce process. At the end of each chapter, there are some questions and a visualization that is pertinent to the chapter content. These are, of course, optional for you, but in my experience I have found that doing questions and exercises called for in a book enhances my learning experience and I get much more out of the reading. If you are doing the exercises, I recommend a journal or dedicated notebook.

I won't bore you with a long introduction about who I am and why I wrote this book. I have been married and divorced twice. My first marriage was short and did not involve children. The divorce itself was simple and inexpensive. My second marriage is the one that gets the lion's share of reference herein, as it is the most recent, the most relevant, and by far the most painful. As for why I wrote this book, I wrote it for me—the person I was almost 10 years ago when my husband told me he was leaving me. Because if I only knew then what I know now, I would have spent more time looking forward and less time looking back. And I wrote it for you, so that you may reap the benefits of my experience, to make this process as pain-free and dignified as it possibly can be.

SECTION 1

Before the Divorce

SCORNED

Chapter One
Grief

You have suffered a monumental loss and you are grieving. You are grieving the loss of your husband, the loss of your marriage, the loss of your way of life. You may even feel that you are grieving the loss of your identity, your very essence. This is a normal process that all women in our position experience.

The grief we feel when losing a partner through separation may not be so different from what people feel when losing a partner through death, because grief is about loss. Death is often sudden and happens without warning; therefore, the impact of surprise makes matters worse in the short term. We may think we have no warning when our partners decide to leave, but when we look back over time, the warning signs were almost always there. Perhaps we chose not to see them. In most cases, when a partner dies, there are external factors to blame; therefore, the rejection factor is different. I can only speak second hand on this issue, as I have no personal experience with the death of a partner. However, the similarity is that you were half of a

7

couple, a Missus with a Mister, and now you are on your own. It isn't only those of us left behind who feel the grief of a lost marriage. Sometimes dissolving the marriage is the right thing for everyone, but somebody has to step up and make that decision. That person has also lost a dream; and, in addition to feeling all the grief, has to be the bad guy. Your husband may have been a scoundrel with an unending wandering eye, or he may have done the right thing for the wrong reasons. Perhaps it was a long time coming and someone had to make the final decision. Some people appear to feel no grief at all, but at some core level they also feel the loss. But this book isn't about them. It's about you.

There are five stages of grief, as introduced in 1969 by Elisabeth Kübler-Ross in her book, *On Death and Dying.* They are denial, anger, bargaining, depression, and acceptance. It is important to fully feel, embrace even, all the stages of grief. These five stages don't always go in order, and they will all revisit at some point. Let yourself feel your grief and find someone that you can share it with. For the majority of us, talking through our grief helps us to understand what we are feeling and move through it. Do not deny yourself the experience. It is not an indulgence. It is a necessary process that we all must go through in order to heal.

My Story
— Like most marriages, mine had its ups and downs. There were periods of peace, contentment, love, and happiness. There were also periods of contempt, disruption, anger, resentment, and outright hostility. Neither of us ever did anything the easy way. We were both stubborn and stuck in patterns we didn't know how to get out of, in some cases even recognize. When I look back on those years, I wonder how we

managed to stay married as long as we did. But like I said, there were some good times, great times, even. We loved each other, and we built a home, a family, and a business together.

My ex-husband was not unfaithful throughout the majority of our marriage. As far as I know, he rarely lied to me and was as committed to the marriage as he could be. I was unhappy for many reasons. That unhappiness was exacerbated by his sometimes careless words and selfish actions. I had a lot of anger and resentment toward him and my life in general. He had his own shortcomings as well, and we were both a little too caught up in our own agendas to help each other out. The last year we were together, I was doing some regression therapy, which brought up mass amounts of old unresolved issues, which he didn't understand and wasn't equipped to deal with.

Even with all that, I thought there was time to fix our relationship. I was convinced that if I just read the right book, or went to the right workshop, or said the right thing in the right way to him, I would get through and all would be well. He (we'll call him Brian), however, had other ideas. He, not being blind, could also see that things were not going well. Instead of looking to fix the problems, he started looking for a way out. He was afraid I would leave him and then he would be alone. Some people cannot imagine anything worse. So he set about making a Plan B. He began looking for a replacement for me. He had a certain criteria, and had more than one candidate.

As luck (or fate) would have it, Brian had a high school reunion, and I selfishly refused to go with him. It was at this reunion that he reconnected with an old friend from high school. He had had a crush on her in high school, but they had just been friends because she was a cheerleader and he was a nerdy D&D guy.

Time and money can change a person's appeal, apparently. She was also in an unhappy marriage, and the stage was set. They began a long-distance relationship, and six months later, he told me he was leaving me for her.

During the time Brian was building a relationship with his "soulmate," he was doing everything he could to disintegrate ours. He lied right to my face about business trips, and reasons to visit his parents, and friends he suddenly had to see. He stayed away from home as much as possible, and when I suggested he spend more time with his sons, he became unreasonably angry. I knew something wasn't right. I even asked him at one point if there was someone else. He denied it then. He agreed to go to a marriage counselor, even though he was committed to leaving me. I started doing everything I thought he wanted me to do, being everything I thought he wanted me to be. We weren't fighting. We were having more sex. Everything was going smoothly, and I was more stressed than at any point in my life. I was trying so hard to be someone else that I lost myself.

About a week before our thirteenth anniversary, Brian took me out for a very nice dinner and when we got home and settled into bed, he dropped the bomb on me. He wanted to divorce me and marry her.

All the pieces came together, and everything started to make sense. I was angry that my husband had been lying to me, but I didn't want our marriage to end. During the following weeks, I went through all the stages of grief. I would begin to think it wasn't real, that he would change his mind (denial). I was sure I could talk him out of it and rehearsed speeches to appeal to his senses (bargaining). I couldn't eat or sleep and functioned on auto-pilot (depression). At random times I would experience brief mini-rages. One night while I was tossing and turning, unable to sleep, I looked over at Brian, snoring contentedly. I smacked him a few times to wake him up and yell at him for having the audacity to be able to sleep (anger). I didn't want him to tell the kids (more denial) or move out until they finished the school year, so I pretended nothing was wrong for the kids. Then on Memorial Day weekend, she came to town so they could find an apartment. That was when I said okay, I'm done. This is really happening (acceptance). In the months (and years) that followed, all of the stages of grief would revisit me in different ways, sometimes taking me quite by surprise.

Denial – This is the first stage of grief that we all go through. This stage is sort of a survival mechanism—a way to cope with the loss. We are in shock, and the world seems surreal. We think this cannot possibly be happening. When your senses are on overload and you are overwhelmed, denial comes in as a soft rescue, albeit a temporary one. It cannot be happening; therefore, it isn't happening. In the days and weeks after Brian told me he was leaving me, I would play it over and over in my head, until the enormity of emotions became too much to handle, and then my brain would just tell me that he wouldn't really go through with it. "He's not really going to leave," I would say. "I can talk him into staying." In the end, it turned out he was more committed to leaving me than he had ever been to staying with me, but I didn't (couldn't) realize that at the time. Denial is nature's way of slowing the pace of the grief so that we can handle it. Some people find it so comfortable there that they never want to leave. It is difficult to be a rational, intelligent person AND remain in denial. Possible, but difficult. It took me a little over a month to realize that the man I had loved with all my heart and soul for the past 18 years was actually leaving me. When your husband files for divorce and moves out, it's a pretty sure thing that he does, indeed, wish to change the nature of your relationship. Once you are released from the paralysis of denial, you can begin taking baby steps toward healing.

For years I was still visited by denial. The denial was not about him leaving and not the denial of raw, gut-wrenching grief. This later denial was leftover fallout from the divorce, and until addressed and dismissed, would still obstruct forward movement. For example, I knew that I would eventually have to sell my house, but I put it off. I tried not to think about it, hoping that I would somehow be able to hang on to it. It was unrealistic denial. The house was too big, too expensive to maintain, and filled with growth-limiting memories. When I finally did sell it, I'll admit it was like going through the divorce all over again. There was a lot of pain, anger, and resentment that came up. Being the only house my kids remembered living in, it was also very difficult for them. For all three of us, the move was excruciating, in large part because I tried to save money by doing a lot of it myself. Did I mention I never did anything the easy way? Once we got through it, however, it was liberating.

At this point, years later, I'm no longer seeing the denial phase come up anymore, at least not related to my marriage and divorce. Good news to share—it really does get better with time.

Anger – A little bit of anger can go a long way. Anger is a normal step in the process of healing. It is also the second stage of grief. Whether you have been left by your partner, you were the one to leave, or it was completely mutual, there is always some level of anger. If you found out your husband was lying to you and sleeping with another woman, then he told you that he wanted to replace you with her, you may have been sent over the top on the anger scale. It is true what they say about a woman scorned. You have a right to be angry. You have a right to be furious. Underneath that anger—what's driving it—is your pain. The anger gives you something tangible to hang on to. It can be almost limitless. You are angry, certainly, at your husband. You are angry at his mistress if there is one. You're angry at any of your friends who may have seen this coming and didn't say anything, at God ("how could You let this happen to me?"). Your husband's family, his co-workers, anyone who doesn't immediately denounce him, all incur your wrath. You have a right (and the need) to express your anger. How you express it, however, is what makes the difference between a graceful ending and a nasty, bitter fight that will cause irreparable damage to both you and your partner, and most regrettably to your children (even if they are already grown and out of the house). Actions like slashing tires and throwing bricks through windows are perhaps not the most productive way to express anger, although they may seem like a good idea at the time. More dangerous and definitely not recommended expressions would include blanket emails detailing your spouse's infidelity, sabotaging your ex-husband at his place of employment, and in the never-never-never category, using your kids as a weapon to punish their father. This is the lowest and meanest way to "get to" your former spouse and has devastating effects on your children and their relationship with both parents. And finally, on the expression of anger—if you feel the need to do physical harm to yourself or others, please put down this book and call someone—anyone—who can help you work through those feelings without doing something everyone will regret.

There are safe ways to express your anger. Vent to friends or a coach or therapist. Write letters to those people with whom you have issue, but don't mail them. Scream into and beat up a pillow. Put on some boxing gloves and wail on a punching bag. Go to a vigorous aerobics class, swim some laps, run. When you physically work out your anger, the effects are two-fold. When you are physically exhausted, the anger takes a back seat, and the endorphins you get from the exercise will make you feel better. In addition, if you are about to have an exchange that you know will make you angry, you can go for a run or a brisk walk beforehand to help yourself get a better handle on it.

You may try to shove your anger deep down in an effort to get rid of it, but this is unhealthy, as it does not go away. Anger is the bad penny of emotions—it keeps showing up, sometimes when you least expect it. When my marriage ended, I felt the full range of emotions—shock, sadness, surprise, depression, self-pity, self-recrimination, etc. Anger, however, was not at the forefront. It would pop up here and there over other (sometimes related, sometimes not) topics, but the underlying anger was down there somewhere—waiting. About a year and a half after my divorce was final, it suddenly appeared. There are two sides to this kind of delay. One side is that your other emotions are less raw and you are better equipped to deal with the anger in a more productive way. The other side, however, is that you probably have other people in your life that will get the brunt of this anger. And they won't understand why you are flinging it at them.

Unresolved anger can show up in many different ways. Your body can only handle so much stress before parts of it start breaking down. Keeping your anger bottled up is dangerous to your health in sometimes unexpected areas. I have read and often refer back to a very interesting book on this subject. It is called *Feelings Buried Alive Never Die*, by Karol K. Truman. In the book, the author goes through many maladies and their respective causes in relation to repressed feelings. I have found it to be spot on in many cases. Once you figure out what physical problems may have arisen from your feelings of frustration, anger, or anxiety, for example, you can process them with the "script." This script was developed by the author to help the reader locate the origin of these negative feelings, name them, and then replace them with their positive counterparts.

Bargaining – This is the third stage of grief. You think you are ready to make a deal. If you still want to try to salvage the marriage, you make promises to yourself and your husband. "I'll do this, that, and the other thing if you will just stay." You'll spend more time with him. You'll have sex more. You'll forgive and forget. You'll learn to cook, or work less, or work more. You'll stop complaining about X, Y, or Z. You'll spend more time doing X, Y, or Z. Ask yourself this: if you weren't willing to do that stuff before, why would you now? There is a possibility that this bargaining with your partner can be effective. If he is leaving you for that one thing that you are now willing to give up because you suddenly realize it was a problem, then perhaps that will do the trick. Think about this: If that ONE THING was a biggie (a veritable deal breaker), like drug or alcohol abuse, or spousal abuse (no, it's not just men who do that), how did you not know it was a problem? There are countless underlying reasons for those things, just as there are for why you let your mom stay for weeks at a time, or don't clean up after yourself, or spend more money than you have, or why you never want to have sex. If that thing you're willing to do is to now accept someone else's bad

behavior, take a pause. If it was intolerable before, why would it be okay now? *Seriously* explore the reasons for the things you are suddenly willing to bargain with before making promises you can't (or maybe shouldn't) keep.

If you are bargaining to keep your marriage, people might ask you why you would want to stay married to a man who wants to leave you, especially if there is another party involved. It is a valid question that only you can answer. You'll get no judgement from me. I spent hours those first few weeks rehearsing speeches to convince Brian not to leave. I felt like I was willing to do anything if he would just stay. It wasn't just the man; it was my life. I had a marriage, a nice home, a family, and we had a business together. I was in shock and not prepared to let go of those things. It doesn't take much imagination to see how things would have gone if I could have brought about his change of heart. I know how I was, and if he had stayed it would not have taken long for the resentment to creep back in and take over. There was a woman out there who he believed was his soulmate. As long as she existed, I seriously doubt that I could ever have felt secure in my marriage.

If you're not bargaining for the future in an attempt to preserve your way of life, you may be trying to bargain for the past, with the "if onlys." If only I had gone with him to that high school reunion. If only I had been better at this, that, or the other thing. If only "that woman" never existed. If only is a waste of time and mental energy. You can't bargain for the past.

Other signs of this bargaining stage involve going to extremes to recover loss (or give the appearance of doing so) or rushing to replace your partner. Recognize and allow yourself the time to get through these stages before making any crazy decisions.

Scorned, Torn And Reborn

Sure, you could have revenge sex with any number of people, but if you want to get through this with your integrity intact, I would strongly advise against it.

Depression – This is the fourth stage of grief. We've gotten past the "if onlys" and are now fully in the present. And we find that it pretty much sucks. We are hit with intense sadness and emptiness. It is natural and normal to go through a period of depression. I long ago lost track of the number of times I went through this particular stage. It would last for a month, or a week, or a couple of hours. That's the funny thing about these grief stages. You don't just do one and check it off your list to move on to the next one. All of them will visit you from time to time, even when you thought they were all behind you. Once you recognize them, they are a bit easier to navigate.

Depression can come as a mild bad mood or it can be completely paralyzing. Some people might spend weeks in bed due to depression. It usually passes and you move on. The problem with depression is that it can become comfortable. If you (or someone you know) are stuck in this phase and it is seriously impairing life function, intervention, even pharmaceutical intervention, may be necessary, most particularly if thoughts of suicide are present. I am not generally a proponent of drugs, but for some people this can be a temporary solution. My first advice would be acupuncture, yoga, meditation, or counseling. Whatever you choose, if your depression is lingering and debilitating, take corrective action of some sort. There are hotlines for every malady imaginable—look in your yellow pages (like we still have those?) or on the internet.

Check with your health insurance for references. Do a little research to choose the best provider for your needs. We'll discuss these solutions in more detail later in the book.

Acceptance – Acceptance is last of the five stages of grief.
This is the point where you say, "Okay. It is what it is, and it is necessary before I can actually move to the path of **recovery**." Don't confuse this acceptance with, "All is well in the world." Acceptance of your situation at this point doesn't mean you are happy or content, or no longer angry, or sad, or depressed, or any of that. It simply means you now recognize you have a new reality that is different from your old one. It means you are now in a place where it is possible for you to begin the healing process. He's gone. He's not coming back. He may be with someone else. That is the new reality, and as uncomfortable as that most surely is, you can now look to the future and begin to make your life work for you on your own terms. It will be a challenge. There will be many ups and downs and uncertainties along the way, but to get to the other side of the mountain, we do have to go over the pass.

If you've been married for a long time, it's probably frightening to now be on your own. You've been one half of a whole, and now you stand solo. You are now the whole. Yes, it may seem daunting to start over at this point, but there is now more freedom than you can imagine to be the person you were born to be. There is nobody to tell you where you will vacation, how you will spend the holidays, what you can or cannot buy. No one to tell you how to wear your hair, how to drive, or what to watch on TV. It is now your opportunity to make life happen for you instead of letting it happen to you. And I'm here to help you.

Exercises

1. In a journal or on your computer, write out your feelings. Try to identify each of the stages of grief as you experience them. This exercise doesn't have to be completed right now; it can and should be an ongoing process.
2. Write down five ways you can express your anger without damaging any property or relationships.
3. What are three things you did simply because your husband wanted you to?
4. What are three things you wanted to do while married but didn't feel like you could?

Visualization

Sit in a quiet place. Get comfortable. Take a deep breath in through your nose and blow it out very slowly through your mouth. With each breath you let out, imagine a part of your body completely relaxing. Start with your head. When you exhale, feel the tension leaving your head. Next, focus on your neck as you exhale. With each breath, move down your body until you get all the way to your toes. Continue to follow your breath as you imagine yourself in a warm bubble bath. The water covers your whole body, and you feel warm and comfortable and relaxed. There is a small box floating in the water. Open it and you will see the word DENIAL. Take the word out and feel what it means to you. Then place the word back in the box and push it aside. Another box appears. You open it and see the word ANGER. Take this word out and feel it. Then place it back in the box and push it aside. The next two boxes to appear will have the words

Rebecca Donovan

BARGAINING and DEPRESSION. Do the same with these words and boxes as you did with the others. The final box will contain the word ACCEPTANCE. When you take out this word, hold it to your heart. Feel the acceptance—of both your current situation and of yourself. Place this word on top of the box and let the box remain with you.

Chapter Two

Betrayal

There are so many different kinds of betrayal, and infidelity is not even in the top three in my opinion. The betrayal of friendship is heartbreaking. The betrayal of your family and children seems unforgivable. To me the worst kind of betrayal is when you trust someone so completely that you give them your heart and soul. You tell them your hopes and dreams and share your most intimate secrets. You lay out on the table all of your greatest fears and deepest insecurities. Then that person you trust uses that information as a weapon to hurt you. THAT is the ultimate betrayal. When this happened to me, it knocked the wind out of me. It felt like a dump truck knocked me down and then backed up and ran over me just for good measure. Betrayal hurts so much because it goes beyond what someone else did to us. It makes us question ourselves—our judgement, our self-worth. How do you come back from that kind of betrayal? How can you ever trust someone again with that much power? How can you look at that person again without wanting to run them over with the dump truck (see **Anger** in the last chapter)? Amazingly, we can recover, even from the worst kind of betrayal. We can forgive. We can learn to trust again. We need to first honor ourselves and be careful about when and how we empower another person with information about what's at the depth of our souls. Honesty is a good thing, but too much honesty too soon is not. Leave a little mystery. Don't bare your entire soul to everyone who is willing to listen. Trust is a gradual process that should be earned.

My Story — For me, the fact that Brian had been sleeping with someone else was not the biggest issue. If I had found out that he had some meaningless affair with some younger woman, I think I could have gotten past it. If he had told me it was a mistake, it meant nothing, he loved me and only me, and it would never happen again, there would have been room to heal. Of course, I can't say that with certainty because that's not what happened. What happened is that he set out to *replace* me. He liked his life and wanted to keep it. He just wanted his life with a new, improved wife. He wanted a wife that would cook and clean more perfectly, have sex whenever he felt like it, and be happy (or at least not complain), regardless of what he said or did. From what I gathered in many hours of conversations with him, he appeared to think it would be a simple matter to just take me out and put someone else in, like buying a new pair of shoes and taking the old ones to Goodwill. One more thing he wanted was to not feel guilty. So he made it all be my fault. For months he and his Plan B would talk on the phone and tell each other how great they each were, and how they would never do A or B and, of course, would always do C and D. Especially D. The more his imaginary scenario took shape, the worse I looked to him, and the more he blamed me for EVERYTHING. He knew my weak points. He knew my insecurities. He knew how to hurt me. When he laid out the way he felt, it was all about my failings, down to the most miniscule detail. And in my state of shock, I believed him. Of all the ways he could have chosen to end our marriage, he chose the one that would hurt me the most. Because he didn't want to feel guilty. For the most part that worked out for him. He had been losing sleep for several months because he felt bad about lying to me. Once he got all that off his chest, and squarely on mine, he slept like a baby. That was the betrayal that almost destroyed me. He knew how to hurt me, and in his twisted logic, he did it so he wouldn't have to feel bad.

So how did I get past this betrayal? I have to admit, it took a long time. There is no magic wand. I had to realize that there were things that I was responsible for and there were a lot of other things that I was not. Over time I regained my self-esteem, rebuilt my self-confidence, and focused on my future. My goal in my coaching practice and in writing this book is to help others do the same thing, only much faster than I did.

Infidelity – The biggest lie men tell their wives (and probably themselves) when their infidelity is discovered, is that they "didn't plan it. It just happened." Somehow they were walking along, minding their own business when they tripped and fell naked into bed with each other. Um, no, it didn't "just happen." My ex-husband used this cliché, as well. It "just happened" because the two of them spent hours on the phone, and then made up stories to tell their spouses, and then he got on an airplane and she got in her car and they went to a pre-arranged meeting place. That amount of planning negates "just happened." They may also try to make it seem like a "love conquers all" kind of thing. They couldn't help themselves. They were drawn together by their love. It was bigger than the both of them. If there was a third party involved in your breakup, these statements may sound familiar. Betraying someone's trust is not a romantic story, regardless of how they may try to spin it to whoever might be listening. It's a conscious decision made for bad reasons, and the consequences are heavy. People are hurt, families are split, children start the long process of her house/his house, friendships are ruined, and on and on. If your pending divorce is due to your own infidelity, you will have additional challenges to face as you try to navigate this process with grace. You are bound to be facing anger, blame, and resentment from all corners of your world. I strongly recommend you speak with a counselor or coach as soon as possible, as this must surely be overwhelming, and you need someone in **your** corner. Regardless of what got us all to this point, the best thing we can do is strive to become a better, stronger version of ourselves and move forward with dignity.

Divorces are inevitable. The only way to be 100 percent sure you will not ever get divorced is to never get married. I am not a proponent of such a thing. Even after two divorces, I still believe marriage is a good thing, whether it lasts forever or not. Even in the best circumstances, divorce is difficult and heart-wrenching. Bringing a third party into the process just makes things harder for everyone. This is where you can insert one of those "if onlys."

When it comes to graceful endings, few things make that more difficult than having to deal with the girlfriend (or boyfriend) who was a part of the destruction of your marriage or partnership. This is a person about whom you might have had violent thoughts of revenge. The last thing you want to do is be civil to her. However, if you have children, or if you have to deal with this person in some other capacity (like if it's your sister or a co-worker), civility is in everyone's best interest—including yours. This will, without a doubt, test what you are made of. You do not need to tell people that your spouse left you for another. People figure that out all on their own. The more you behave with dignity and grace, the better you look and the worse your former partner looks. There is a small amount of vindication in that. And as for the "other," they have their own issues to deal with. Stepping into someone else's life is not as easy as they thought it might be. They will have to live with the whispers and stink eyes. Most people won't say anything about it to you right away, but over time people will let you know how they felt about what happened. I still run into folks occasionally who know Brian's wife and tell me they can't believe he chose her. It's been long enough now that those comments don't really affect me much one way or the other. But sometimes, still, just a little smile will come up. I am human after all.

Even if you never meet this other person, the fact of their existence raises the levels of anger, disappointment, and heartache exponentially. I had a friend whose husband was having an affair for a number of years, and this affair led to the demise of the marriage. After a year, this friend was still printing pictures from his email correspondence with the "other woman" and getting herself all worked up over and over again. She was keeping the pain close to her heart by constantly revisiting the past. What happened, happened. You must choose to put it in the past where it belongs or it will continue to make you crazy. This is not an easy task. It takes strength of character. No matter how much you wish for it, you cannot change what has gone before. It will stay with you until you choose to move past it.

Rebecca Donovan

Justification – With enough skill and practice, one can justify anything. Most people can justify the small things, like little white lies, being late, missing commitments, or taking home office supplies. Many others can justify the big things, like being mean to people, cheating on their taxes, and being unfaithful. Usually this justification goes along with blame. If you have the ability to make everything you do someone else's fault, it is quite easy to justify your actions. At the end of the day, when you look at yourself in the mirror, there is no justification for doing what you know is not right. No matter how hard you try to get around it, it is not okay to lie, steal, or cheat. You learned that from your mom or in bible school or at the very least kindergarten. Don't try to justify bad behavior on your part because he justified bad behavior on his part. You can handle this breakup with dignity and integrity. You will feel so much better about yourself in the long run.

Karma – Time wounds all heels. We all have made some contribution to the demise of our relationships, but sometimes the other person *really* was a giant ass. I am a firm believer in "what goes around comes around." Often people have an affair with someone and leave their spouse because they think the new person is so much better. They have only seen them at their best and only for short periods of time. It's easy to be sweet and compassionate and funny and wonderful for a few hours at a time. Living with someone is hard. You see all their warts, smell all their smells, get the brunt of their bad moods, and are privy to their insecurities, phobias, and neuroses. Everyone has these things, and the spouse who thought that greener grass was filled with roses will come to find there are also thorns. They will, of course, want you to think everything is great, because nobody likes "I told you so." If you have kids, or mutual friends, they will generally bring you up to speed on the real deal. People who hurt other people with total disregard for anything other than their own gain rarely get what they really want, even though on the surface it seems that they do. They are always unsatisfied and looking for something to fill the voids that exist in their own hearts.

Secrets – Some people are incredibly talented at keeping secrets. There are individuals who have found out after years of marriage that their spouse is gay, or a crossdresser, or has an addiction of some sort that they kept hidden. A surprising number can keep an affair going for years without being detected. If this was the case for you, you may be thinking, *How could I have **not** known?* It makes you feel foolish and doubt yourself. Don't. This person has been keeping this thing a secret for a long time. Some secrets have been kept longer than you have known them. When you look back, maybe you can see that something was "off" and maybe now that you know the truth, it make sense. On the other hand, they may have been so good at hiding their "other life" that there were no clues at all. Whether coming into this knowledge caused the breakup or just happened peripherally, it's not your fault that you didn't know. Now that you do know, only you can decide if the secret is something you can accept, support, forgive, or all three.

Reconciliation – You want this to be a graceful ending, but maybe you are asking yourself if it really does have to be the end of your marriage. Beyond your own denial, is there a real chance that this whole divorce thing is just a wake-up call? Is your husband asking the same question? Maybe after he thinks about it, he changes his mind. Maybe asking for the divorce made it all too real and Plan B was not looking so enticing. There are cases where people are on the brink of divorce, or actually divorced, and then discover a way to make the relationship work. Those people who make public statements about it in blogs or books tend to talk about it pretty soon after they get back together, so the longevity factor is missing. Not so long ago, I briefly dated a man who was in the process of getting divorced. He had married his current wife very soon after his first wife had passed. This, I'm sure, added to the problems he was experiencing with the new wife. At the time I met him he was 100 percent sure he wanted the divorce. He had moved out, gotten a lawyer, and filed the paperwork. They are now happily back together. This is one really good reason, by the way, not to date for a while after your divorce, and a bigger reason not to date someone else who is not yet divorced. If you are considering reconciliation, then you are still in the right place with this book. A long, drawn out, bitter divorce does not generally make the heart grow fonder. Think twice and then think more about this. It can't be just you—both of you have to REALLY want to work this out. You have to be willing to go above and beyond what you were willing to do before. Remember what I said about bargaining. If you have children, they will most likely be fans of the reconciliation. However, this is not to be taken lightly, because the worst thing is to create a see saw to further confuse and alienate your children. It's not my intention to discourage this re-mating, only to caution against impulsiveness. Only you can decide if you are able to forgive and forget. If there was another woman involved, that means you have to forgive and then act like you forget, because you are not going to forget. There will be that thing in the back of your mind every time he goes on a business trip (especially if that's when he conducted the affair), or calls to say he's working late, or just wants to spend a little time by himself. It will be a long and arduous process to get back to where you were. Once you have mulled it over, talked it out, and gotten some professional counseling, if you are BOTH truly committed to this reconciliation, then I applaud the effort and wish you luck.

Trust – Learning to trust again is a tall order once you have been betrayed in your relationship. Not only if you are thinking of reconciling, but learning to trust again, in any capacity, is difficult. Many of us have trust issues that were around long before we ever entered into the relationship; and, unless we make some changes, will be around forever more. These issues draw us to certain people who, it turns out, can't be trusted. It is a vicious cycle that we have to break if we are ever going to have the healthy, loving relationships that we deserve. There is a book that has been monumental in my personal healing process. *Calling In "The One,"* written by Katherine Woodward Thomas, helped me to discover some of my own trust issues and their origins and then how to release them. This is also an area where a therapist or life coach can be very beneficial.

Blame and Responsibility – These are two sides of the same coin, yet very different. Blame is the negative side. It is a way to make someone else wrong, in order to somehow vindicate ourselves, or to become the victim. Responsibility is the positive side. This is the side where you own your thoughts, feelings, and actions. Both you and your husband have responsibility for what happened and what didn't happen in your marriage.

Rebecca Donovan

You cannot place all of the blame on your former partner any more than you can accept all of the blame yourself. There was a short period of time following my big breakup when I did just that. I believed with all my being that the whole thing was my fault. Why would I think such a ridiculous thing? Because that's what the man I loved told me. He blamed me for everything— my unhappiness, his unhappiness, every problem our kids had, every argument we had, his infidelity. Could my flaws be so powerful that they would cause *every single* problem in a marriage? No, of course not. And neither could yours. If your husband is attempting to place all the blame on you in an effort to make himself feel better, don't let him get away with that. He has to own his responsibility for his thoughts, feelings, and actions as well. It's very sad that in many relationships the parties involved truly do believe that every problem is the other person's fault. It is extremely limiting to never feel the need for reflection. You can't change the past, but unless you reflect on it and learn from it, you will be stuck in it. That is what blame does. It paralyzes your growth. We all make mistakes and change our minds, and that's the only way we can grow—spiritually, mentally, emotionally. Accept your *responsibility* but not the blame. There are so many factors that go into the dissolution of a marriage, just as there are to keep one going. It is extremely rare that one half of the couple caused all the problems. I have spoken to quite a few people who were at this stage in the breakup, the one where they believe they had behaved impeccably while their former partner was a one-man band of destruction. In order to recover from this loss and move forward, you must stop playing the blame game. You can't continue to blame someone else for your actions, emotions, feelings, or continued lack of happiness. Those are yours. You have the power to change them.

Scorned, Torn And Reborn

"Wait a minute," you might say. "What about when he cheated on me? What about when he got drunk and said mean things to me?" Yes, without a doubt, our former partners have done and said mean things to us. And most of us have done the same. We made a choice about what actions to take in reaction to his actions. He made a choice about what to do in reaction to our reactions. All these reactions cause more reactions that soon spiral out of control. At some point we have to stop blaming and reacting and just accept what's ours and how we want to move forward. Once you've done this, you can focus on creating a better life for yourself. I don't mean to say this is a simple and easy thing to do. It isn't. Your former partner may have done A LOT of mean stuff, with far-reaching consequences. You can sit back and coast smugly on the blame express, fueled by your supportive friends and family who all tell you it was **his** fault. Unfortunately, that doesn't get us anywhere. At some point, in order to move forward, we have to let go of the blame.

Don't be surprised if your former partner has trouble accepting his own responsibility. I know people who bent over backwards for years to do everything they could to be completely above board at every turn, to be completely fair. In the end their former spouses still blamed them. While it would be nice if they didn't, it's not relevant to how you feel about yourself. I feel some pity for those people because they will always be stuck in first gear. You, however, have the option to keep shifting gears until you're at cruising speed.

I am a huge believer in personal responsibility. You are in charge of your thoughts, actions, feelings, and happiness. Nobody is responsible for your happiness but you. Let me repeat that. **Nobody is responsible for your happiness but you.** Once you place your happiness in the hands of another person, you are no longer in control of it. There is a lovely story in the book, *The Mastery of Love,* by Don Miguel Ruiz, about a man who didn't believe in love. He spent most of his life unsuccessfully searching for love, finally declaring that it just didn't exist. He was very smart and became a scholar, arguing his cynical stance on love and his fatalistic view of marriage with anyone who would listen. One day he happened upon a beautiful woman who was upset because she also believed that love did not exist. She had been in a marriage that had turned sour and was convinced it would always be like that. This man and woman were drawn together by their shared belief and became good friends. Their friendship and mutual respect grew and evolved. Upon reflection one day, the man was struck by the thought that maybe he loved her. Perhaps love did exist after all. When he told her of his feelings, she agreed and told him she felt the same way. They became lovers and lived together in happiness. Then, one night a miracle happened. He was looking at the stars, his heart full of love, when the most beautiful star came down from the sky and into his hands. His soul then merged with the star and he was filled with happiness. He rushed home in excitement and placed the star in his lover's hands. Once he placed his happiness in her hands, she was overwhelmed by the responsibility and had a moment of doubt. The star fell from her hands and broke apart. The man went back to believing love didn't exist.

When you make someone else responsible for your happiness, it is unlikely that they will be able to succeed in the job. Because your happiness is your job. You cannot make another person be happy. I live in and fully understand the real world. We are affected by the actions of other people, particularly those we care about. It hurts us that someone we love would knowingly cause us pain, or actually stop loving us for whatever reason. Most people (except perhaps some cave monks, and possibly an occasional middle school administrator) feel the thoughts, emotions, and actions of other people. It is one of the things that make us human. However, once the initial surprise/shock/appall/pain wears off, you alone must determine how you want to look at the situation and how you want to move forward. Once you realize this, you are both empowered and maybe a bit frightened. You cannot accept this new idea and remain a victim. Statements like "you make me angry" or "he made me lie to him" don't fly here. Stop letting life happen *to* you and start making it happen *for* you. Whether or not you recognize it, you are in control of your destiny and responsible for your choices. By the way, doing nothing is also a choice, as is being a victim. They are just not very good choices.

Being betrayed by someone you loved and trusted is deeply wounding. If that person is also now telling you that you are being replaced, that is certainly pouring salt into the wound. Keeping your head up and behaving with dignity and integrity is a lot to ask. This is the reality. The past cannot be altered. What we can do right now is to sort out responsibilities and let go of blame. It is one step of many that will get us where we want to go.

Exercises

1. List three problems in your marriage for which you were at least partially responsible. This is not for self-blame or recrimination. The purpose is to recognize your part so that you can grow from this experience.
2. List three things that your husband blames, or has blamed, you for unfairly.
3. Think of a time when you made someone else responsible for your happiness and/or someone else made you responsible for theirs.
4. List three things you can do to take control of your own happiness.

Visualization

Sit in a quiet place. Get comfortable. Take a deep breath in through your nose and blow it out very slowly through your mouth. With each breath you let out, imagine a part of your body completely relaxing. Start with your head. When you exhale, feel the tension leaving your head. Next, focus on your neck as you exhale. With each breath, move down your body until you get all the way to your toes. Continue to follow your breath as you imagine yourself on the edge of a bluff, looking down at a rocky beach. A gust of wind picks up and you feel vulnerable on the edge. You reach for the hand of the person standing next to you. You immediately feel safe and protected. Who is there with you? There may be several people there. Relish what it feels like to have those trusted people with you.

Chapter Three
Self-Image

"What lies behind us and what lies before us are tiny matters compared to what lies within us."
— Ralph Waldo Emerson

The way we think about ourselves has taken a big hit with these new circumstances in our lives. It would be almost impossible to not be knocked off center by the revelation that our way of life is about to drastically change. Explore with me some of the feelings we are experiencing and also some ways to make sense of them to turn ourselves toward feeling better.

My Story — I have to admit that I was devastated by the breakup. As I said before, I initially took on the blame and felt horrible about myself. And once he was on a roll, Brian just went with it, fueling that fire of sorrow with rejection, failure, and guilt. In those first weeks, I was sure I would never be whole again. My entire life was being taken from me. I thought the sun would never shine again. I was a mess. My entire focus was on how horrible it all was. How could he do this to me, to our family? As time went by, it turned out that I was still breathing and the sun did come up every single day without fail. I slowly began to realize that I was worth more on my own than I thought. I could take care of myself, the kids, and the dog. I read a lot of self-help books, joined a support group, and got some therapy. These actions helped me to see myself in a different way, and to see my husband in a different way. I had a long way to go, but not just because of the breakup. I had a lot of baggage coming in. Brian had told me that every single problem we had in our marriage was a direct result of my insecurities. While that was, um, harsh, he wasn't 100 percent wrong. My insecurities were definitely responsible for many of the problems I had in our marriage. His problems were his alone.

Rejection – Any kind of rejection is hard to take. Fear of rejection is one of the biggest fears that we have. For many people this fear keeps them from ever doing anything meaningful. Getting fired from a job, getting blown off by a friend, the first time your kids prefer their friends' company to yours—all of these forms of rejection leave us feeling somehow...less. But being cast off by a lover—that is the big mother of rejection. You experience disappointment, unfulfilled expectations, resentment, and then the one that will suck the very life out of you—hate. It has always amazed me how quickly people can go from love to hate. It turns out that a broken heart is all in your head—literally. The part of the brain that gets turned on when we are in love is the same part of the brain that freaks out when that love is taken away. This is the part of the brain that is responsible for all the crazy things people do following a lover's rejection. Some people do really bad things in a blast of revenge that they later regret, maybe while sitting in jail. Learning to recognize these powerful urges spawned by rejection is key to finding less damaging avenues for letting out your frustrations. When your brain is fighting against what you are trying to accomplish, then integrity becomes all about impulse control.

Failure – Many people (you may be one of them) consider divorce to be the ultimate failure. I personally do not feel this way. I bristle slightly when I hear people say, "He had two failed marriages" or "My marriage was a failure." Life is full of changes, and divorce is one of the big ones, but change does not automatically mean failure. Would you say that Blockbuster was a failed business? What about VCRs? Were they a failed product? Eight-track tapes? Well, yes, maybe that one. It's true that when we get married we expect it to be forever (at least most of us do). But people change. Relationships change. Circumstances change. There are as many reasons for the demise of a relationship as there are relationships. Are two miserable people who remain married engaged in a successful marriage? Where there is abuse, alcoholism, and adultery, should a marriage remain intact simply to avoid that "failure?" I don't think it should. If two people are not happy being married to each other, they have three clear options: Option 1: Get help to try to fix the problems (not always possible). Option 2: Separate. Option 3: Do nothing, and remain unhappy. My marriage was not happy for quite some time. While I opted for Option 1, I didn't pursue that avenue wholeheartedly until it was too late. Option 3 was where we stayed for a couple of years, although there were certainly many happy times interspersed in there. Finally, my husband opted for Option 2. He had his own reasons, and ultimately he decided he would be happier elsewhere. We wanted different things from marriage. We did not discuss these before the wedding, assuming, like most people, that if we loved each other, then everything else would magically fall into place. Well, guess what? It didn't. When

Rebecca Donovan

I reflect on the past in regard to my former husband, I wish him the best and hope that the change he decided to make will lead to his continued happiness. Do I believe he behaved badly and could have done things differently that would have ultimately easier for everyone? Yes, I do. I don't condone his actions, but knowing him as I do, I understand them.

Guilt — This one is huge. If you are like the vast majority of the population in this country, you feel a lot of guilt. Most of us are raised on it. A close relative of self-blame, guilt really doesn't have a purpose unless you do something about it. Just feeling it has no value. Holding on to guilt is extremely stressful and will eventually make you sick. Why am I talking about guilt here, when he was the one who abandoned you? Maybe, you did something, too. If you are feeling guilty because you had an affair, or you weren't fully present for your husband and/or family, or you were unreasonably jealous, or, or, or.... Do what you need to do to make amends. This may simply be to apologize and ask for forgiveness. You may not get it, but once you have done what you can do (you can obviously never change the past), forgive yourself and let go of the guilt. Before you go confessing to cleanse your soul, however, take a pause to think it through. Will this revelation help or harm the relationship going forward? Your marriage may be over, but there is still a relationship to consider, especially if you have children. The best thing to do now is to accept the consequences of your actions, learn from the experience, and move forward.

A cautionary note about guilt: when I say make amends, I do not mean sacrifice your future to do so. Do not throw in a bunch of extra stuff and money, thinking that will make the hurt go away. Those extra stock funds, the valuable art work, and the vacation home are assets you may not have surrendered had you been thinking clearly and taken your time with the divorce. If you are living in an efficiency apartment while your former partner is driving the Mercedes and living in the five-bedroom house, it may dawn on you that you gave up too much to ease your conscience or just to get it over with. You will be feeling less guilty later and may regret making financial decisions based on raw emotion. This regret invariably leads to resentment. Do not let your resentment over your own guilty conscience and bad financial decisions affect the way you handle your relationship with your ex. This is particularly important if you have children.

On the other side of the equation is the guilt your husband must surely be experiencing. He may be willing, eager even, to part with some extras as part of his guilty conscience. Sometimes when a man is eager to move on and set up housekeeping with the new woman in his life, he will try to rush the divorce through. That's what happened in my case. Don't let him do this. You can go through the process at the pace that works for both of you, not just for him. Be reasonable, but don't let him steamroll you. You think you know him, but I have to tell you that people can become unrecognizable during a divorce. He may tell you he's giving you something and then you find out he was manipulating you. Take your time, read everything twice, and then think it through, preferably with a professional advisor. In later chapters we will discuss some of the practical legal and financial aspects of this adventure.

Victim – Sometimes you really are the victim. It's quite rare, however, that you become a victim without some level of consent on your part. Don't get me wrong. I'm not saying that anyone *deserves* to be used, abused, or lied to. What I'm saying is that we put a message about ourselves out there and what comes to us generally mirrors how we feel about ourselves. As we'll talk about later in the book, this is the time to reflect on how we got into these intolerable situations in the first place. Now that we are out, we need to figure out how to NOT ever go there again. It is a process, and usually not a quick one. Buckle down for the long haul and be honest with yourself so that you can overcome being the victim. A friend in my divorce support group once said that staying in her broken relationship was like having someone stab her over and over again, and then finally figuring out that she needed to get out from under the knife. It doesn't have to be about physical or emotional abuse. It can be that everyone you are with treats you with disrespect or is a perfectionist or a narcissist or is manipulative. You are trying to figure out what the common factor is in all these people you are involved with that do the same thing. The common factor is you. You do not have to be the victim. You owe it to yourself to *not* be the victim.

Self-Respect — In order to have integrity, you must also have self-respect. And vice versa. They go hand in hand. Sure, it's easy to *say* you need to have self-respect. It's harder to really get there. If you are coming out of an abusive relationship, chances are high that it wasn't your first. Unless you make some changes in how you see yourself, it won't be your last. This is a pattern we get into with being a victim. There are so many books and articles and blogs written to help you regain your self-respect after being in an abusive relationship. When I say the word abusive, I am not just talking about physical abuse. Much more commonplace is emotional abuse. It can be so subtle that you don't even recognize it as abuse, but it tears you down just the same. You start to believe what the abuser wants you to believe—that you are not worthy, that you can't do better, and that you have to put up with it. Well guess what? You are, you can, and you don't. Not anymore.

Any relationship that has gone bad, with or without abuse, can have detrimental effects on our self-respect. When we are angry, lonely, frustrated, confused, etc., we say and do things that in hindsight we wish we wouldn't have. Sometimes we really hurt those that we love. Once said, harsh words can never be taken back. Hasty actions cannot be undone. Unfortunately, we can't change the past. We can only live our present and move forward into the future.

I also recommend working with a good therapist or life coach to help you with this. The two are different, and I will go into more detail in the next chapter. Take the advice you get from the books and articles that you read and your therapist or coach. Do the exercises they recommend. Keep company with positive people who LIKE you. Hang out with your dog. Do things that you know you are good at. Try new things that you think you'll enjoy. When deciding how to act or what to say in a certain situation, think about what will make you feel good about yourself. Vengeance rarely makes us respect ourselves. Behave in a way that will help you build your self-confidence and self-respect.

Achievements – Recognize these, no matter how tiny they may be. "I got out of bed today." "I fed the dog." "I got myself to work." "I showed up for library duty at the school." "I remembered to eat lunch." "I paid the bills." "I made dinner for the kids." You get the idea. With the advancement of time, these achievements will get more substantial, but always remember to recognize them and give yourself credit for each and every one. Some days you look back and think that you accomplished nothing. It isn't true. Count your achievements. Write them down. Achieve more tomorrow.

When you are feeling emotionally devastated, the world seems to pass you by in a fog. The lack of food and lack of sleep can add to your wounds to turn you into a red-nosed, tear-smudged zombie. In this stage, everyday tasks become enormous obstacles. You want nothing more than to stay under the covers or sit in the closet all day, but life, indeed, does go on and you are needed to participate in it. The children still have to be fed, the laundry still has to be done, and that stupid Cub Scout project you cannot imagine why you volunteered for still looms large in your very near future. Getting from point A to point B each day when you are so emotionally raw takes an incredible amount of energy and motivation. Give yourself credit for these achievements. They will get easier, I promise.

Ability — We need to do a bit more recognizing here. This relationship didn't work and there are probably a thousand reasons why. That doesn't mean you don't have the ability to have another one. You will have a better one, in fact, because you will have learned so much. You do have the ability to have a meaningful, fulfilling relationship. If your former partner tries to tell you differently, don't listen to him. He has only his perspective, and there are always two sides to any story. There probably is some work to be done on your part to get past the things in your life that have been blocking you so far, but you do have the ability to love, laugh, and be happy again. What's more, you deserve those things. Accept that fact.

This is the part where you may say, "Yeah, right." When your relationship has just ended, it may seem impossible that you will ever be content, much less happy, and laugh again. Love again? Forget it. You do know that you never want to go through this whole breaking up process again. The thing about the human heart, however, is that it is unbelievably resilient. It does heal and it does need to share. Start out small. Connect with friends and family and, of course, always, your dog or other pet. Romance will come in to your life again—maybe sooner, maybe later—and you can make sure you are in a better place to give and receive love, laughter, and happiness again. In the meantime, focus on less risky relationships. I mention my dog quite often in this book. She has absolutely been my best friend, and I always know she loves me unconditionally. She knows when I want to be alone, and she knows when I need a hug, and she has at times been the one constant in my life.

Acknowledge – Though your perspective may be clouded at this point, there were many good things about your relationship and your partner. Acknowledge these things. Write a letter to your husband acknowledging him. Send it or not—up to you—but write it. I sent my ex-husband an email after the divorce, thanking him for his contributions to making me a better person. I got this idea from a wonderful book I was reading at the time, *The Spiritual Divorce* by Debbie Ford. Every person with whom you have a relationship has something of value that they give you that can never be taken away. They are each part of who you are. Some of the things on my list were my children, his teaching me about history, encouraging me to travel to places I would not have gone on my own, and his challenging me intellectually. This exercise is not meant to bring up reasons to hang on to the past or be sad about the loss. These are things that someone who loved you (and whom you loved) gave you that you have **not** lost, and never will. If you do send the letter, you may get a nice response back. It took some time, but I did get a very moving response back from my ex-husband. It was empowering to see his acknowledgement of my contributions to his life. You may not receive a response, but that's not the point. This is about what you have gained from your relationship with your partner that you take with you always.

In the heat of the battle, so to speak, this acknowledgement gives you something positive to think about. If you do send it, it may take a little wind out of his puffy, angry sails and make him think of you in a more positive way as well. If your husband is especially unreasonably bitter at this point, you may want to hold off sending it. You don't need the negativity of a potentially hateful response to derail you.

It may be too soon for you to write such a letter, let alone send it. If your emotions are too raw right now and writing this type of letter seems impossible, then wait until you are ready. Everyone must move through this process at their own pace. Instead, for everything you feel that you have lost, or are losing, try to think of one thing that you get to keep, something that cannot be taken away.

Appreciation – Take the time to appreciate what you have. This is very important at a time when you are thinking so heavily on what you have lost. Are you still healthy? Appreciate this and protect it (more about this in the next chapter). Do you have children? Appreciate them and let them know that you do. Appreciate your friends and let them help you. Appreciate your family and let them help you. Appreciate your dog. Appreciate the beauty around you—the sun, and the trees, and the flowers. Look around you and you will find an infinite array of appreciable items. When you are feeling particularly low, take out a piece of paper and write down a list of the things you still have in your life that you are grateful for. I write one full page every day on the things I appreciate. You will be amazed once you get started just how many there are. I recently did a whole page just on coffee. This appreciation will take you a long way toward your next goal.

Attitude – This is a big one. You cannot control what has happened or how much it has hurt you. You can, however, control the way you choose to think about your situation from this day forward. I was very hurt by the breakup of my marriage. Like most people, I thought my marriage would last forever. I thought that somehow the problems we faced would work out. But, clearly, they didn't. Once I accepted the facts, I had a choice to make. I could wallow in self-pity, resentment, and anger and become a bitter old woman. Or, I could change my attitude and start the healing process. While the improvement of your attitude is tied to the acceptance, you don't automatically get a great attitude by acceptance, but, again, it is the first step. Once you accept what IS, consider how you feel about it. Let yourself feel what you feel. Your feelings are real, and no one, including you, can make you not feel them. It's what you DO with your feelings that makes the difference. It takes a little practice. When you haven't slept, and you are not eating properly, and you've abandoned your exercise routine, it's hard to have a great attitude, but still possible to have one that's not terrible. As you drag your body out of bed, say to yourself, "Thank you for this day. Thank you for the opportunity to make today better than yesterday." It might sound a little hokey to you, but it is a good start, and it has worked for me. As you

45

consciously improve your attitude, the things that create or contribute to the bad attitude tend to diminish. There is no magic quick fix to these circumstances in which you now find yourself. It is a process that takes time, and there will be many ups and downs. The key is to keep plodding forward. Make a conscious decision that you WANT to feel better, and you will begin to see improvements in your attitude about everything. Trust me, it can be done. I did it, and I started out in a pretty low place.

Believe – Believe in yourself. You can get through this, and you can do it with your dignity intact. This is for no one more than yourself and your children if you have them. Believe that you can get through the next hour. Believe that you can get up and go to work tomorrow. Believe that there is a plan in place and your life will be better than it was before. There are people in your life who believe in you, too. Spend some time with these people and listen to what they say. Believe in better tomorrows, and you will be able to make them happen.

Change – Some people thrive on change. Others can barely tolerate it. For the majority of people, change is much easier to deal with when it is their idea. The truth is that change is the one constant. Without change there is no growth. Without growth, we stagnate and wither. Good will come from every form of change. It may take a long time to realize what that good was, but it is there. The more you allow yourself to see that good, the easier the change will be. Eckhart Tolle wrote in his book *A New Earth*, "Some changes may look negative on the surface but you will soon realize that space is being created in your life for something new to emerge." When the news of my upcoming divorce finally sunk in, the coming changes seemed enormous, none of them good. *Everything about my life is going to change,* I thought. *Nothing will ever be the same. It's going to be horrible!!!!*

There were, certainly, many changes. But not everything about my life changed, and not all of the changes were bad. Many of my perceived changes had to do with the assumed perception of other people. My external identity would be different. As it turned out, that didn't matter, because I found out who my friends were and who were just acquaintances. This is very good information to have—a positive change. I no longer had someone telling me what to do or what I should have done but didn't. Positive change. I no longer had someone telling me how to wear my hair, how to exercise, how to dress, how to drive. More positive changes. I no longer felt I had to justify how I spent my time or money. I could go where I wanted to go on vacation. My self-esteem improved. I had time to spend with girlfriends, and the time I had with my children was more meaningful because much of the stress I felt in my home was gone. I felt free to explore my spirituality and I could write, finally, which is what I wanted to do all my life. There were, of course, negative changes, but with each day that passed I found that the good ones overshadowed the bad ones.

Everyone's self-confidence takes a hit during a breakup. When you add in rejection, feelings of failure, and guilt, it is a sad mixture, indeed. Start by believing in yourself. Recognize your unique abilities and your achievements, however small they may sometimes seem. Your positive attitude will prevail as you look forward with gratitude for the things you have. Appreciate all the good in your life—your children, your family, and your friends. Notice the beauty that surrounds you in all its forms. Embrace the changes that are to come.

Exercises

1. List five things you accomplished today. They can be small or large.
2. List five things you have to be grateful for. Again, they can be small or large.
3. List five positive changes that come with this divorce. They don't have to be big changes.

Visualization

Sit in a quiet place. Get comfortable. Take a deep breath in through your nose and blow it out very slowly through your mouth. With each breath you let out, imagine a part of your body completely relaxing. Start with your head. When you exhale, feel the tension leaving your head. Next, focus on your neck as you exhale. With each breath, move down your body until you get all the way to your toes. Continue to follow your breath as you imagine something you are grateful for that can never be taken away. Think of as many things as you can and feel the gratitude and appreciation surround you like a warm blanket.

Chapter Four
Self-Care

Emotional trauma in your life inevitably causes physical trauma because you are completely out of balance. It is essential for you to take care of your body if you want to regain your balance and navigate this breakup with any level of grace. Even if you want to skip the grace, it's still important to pay attention to the messages your body is sending you.

My Story — As you probably know by now, I was in pretty bad shape immediately following my husband's big revelation. I went on what I call the Divorce Diet. I couldn't eat. I couldn't sleep. I lost 10 pounds in a few weeks. After the first week of no sleep, I knew I needed help. I don't like pharmaceuticals of any kind, so sleeping pills were not my first choice. I started with my acupuncturist. She did some relaxation techniques for me and gave me some natural sleep aids to take. What she did that was most beneficial was to listen to me. She was the first person I really talked to about what was going on, and while it wasn't her job to be my therapist, she was there for me. Unfortunately, the natural stuff didn't do the trick, although I did feel more hopeful when I left her office.

Still desperate for sleep that wouldn't come, I went to my GP for a prescription. She wrote me a prescription for a 30-day supply of Ambien without asking me a single question. I know I looked really bad, so I was surprised that she didn't care enough to have a conversation. I changed doctors after that, but in the short term, the Ambien did the trick. I was able to sleep, and it made a huge difference in how I felt.

Eating was another matter. It was difficult for me to eat anything, as I had zero appetite. And exercise was out of the question since I wasn't eating or sleeping well. As a reasonably intelligent person, I realized this was not a good combination. I took the Ambien for about a week and then off and on for a couple of weeks until I was able to sleep more on my own. I concentrated on eating more, taking my vitamins, and doing a little yoga at home.

Life had been stressful for a while preceding the big announcement. My body was completely tied in knots. I had been experiencing excruciating pain in my neck, upper back, and shoulders for months. Someone recommended a great chiropractor, who is my hero to this day. He not only got rid of that pain, but helped me with another chronic hip problem I had dealt with for years.

All of these actions got me back on track physically, which boosted my ability to handle the emotional issues.

Physical Health – Few events are as stressful as the breakup of a marriage or long-term relationship. And there is nothing quite as effective as stress to destroy your health—if you let it. If you wish to behave in a rational manner and go through this with dignity and grace, then you must take care of your health. It is more important than ever to do what is necessary to maintain good health. I am a big proponent of natural health and tend to shy away from traditional Western medicine and the associated doctors. However, I do go every year for a full physical with a "regular" doctor and recommend you do, too. Don't stop there, however. Take a proactive approach to your health by eating healthy foods and exercising. Don't drink too much coffee or alcohol, and while this may not be the best time to quit smoking, try to cut back or at least take care not to smoke more. Equally important to your health are relationships with other people (or at least your dog or cat). Do not isolate yourself like a monk in a cave. Be with people and talk to them. Without your own good health, you are not in a good position to take care of anyone else, like your children if you have them.

Mental Health – It is certainly as important to tend to your mental health as it is your physical health. Do things that will take your mind off of your circumstances, if only briefly. If you don't have a pet, maybe consider adopting one, or perhaps just temporarily foster a homeless cat or dog. It helps us gain perspective if we have someone or something else to take care of. Of course, if you are overwhelmed already, taking on that new responsibility may be too much. Only you know what your bandwidth is. Plenty of studies have been done that show us it is not good to be all alone all the time. Get off the couch and out of the house. Visit with friends. Do not wallow in self-pity or it will become your life.

Sleep – This is essential. You cannot function at all if you are not sleeping. You certainly can't focus on the things you need to focus on to successfully get through this difficult time. There are many natural ways to help get you to sleep. Some ideas to try: herbal teas before bedtime, a relaxing warm bath, meditating before bed, self-love (wink-wink), focusing on one positive thing—story, memory, etc., turn off all electronics at least an hour before bed, and limit caffeine and alcohol. If none of these things is working, then I would suggest getting something from your physician. As I said previously, I am not generally a proponent of drugs of any kind, but if this is what you need to do in the SHORT TERM to get some sleep, then by all means, do it. Again, you cannot function if you are not sleeping.

Eat – When your stomach has turned inside out and the very thought of food makes you nauseated, it is indeed difficult to eat. As I said, I lost 10 pounds in the first month after my breakup because I couldn't eat. This is not healthy, however, and you can't do it for very long. Between lack of sleep, lack of food, and the stress you are feeling, your body can't help but start shut-down procedures. If you are not eating, you are robbing your body of any chance of recovery. Try small portions frequently throughout the day—a few goldfish crackers and a piece of cheese or a cup of yogurt and some fruit. Make sure you get enough protein to keep your brain functioning properly. Your already compromised digestive system can handle small amounts of food more easily. Try to steer away from fast food. Most of that is not good for you anyway. More detail follows in the next section.

Nutrition – You are what you eat! This is the starting point for good health. What you put in and on your body makes all the difference in how you feel. I went to a writing workshop recently at a lovely retreat center in Austin. The center is devoted to purity and balance and vegan consumption. There is a restaurant there that serves only vegan cuisine. After lunch I felt satisfied, yet so light and well, just good. Let me clarify—I am not vegan. I am not even remotely vegetarian. But I am a proponent of healthy food choices, and when I eat natural (without antibiotics and preservatives), organic, etc., I feel better.

I first began studying nutrition when my sons were in elementary school. In reading a multitude of books and talking with a child development specialist, I learned that processed foods and icky things like pesticides and growth hormones and antibiotics can cause or exacerbate developmental and behavioral issues. Out went the processed foods, the high-fructose corn syrup, and hydrogenated oils. In came the fresh (or at least frozen) vegetables and fruit, natural meat, and what organics I could reasonably get. There is a reason why the label on a can of green beans can't list any nutrients—there aren't any. They were long since removed by the extreme heat used to process the vegetables. I can't say I'm a purist. I hear raw milk is the way to go and goat's milk is better than cow's. I don't have the time or energy to go out and find a farm to provide these things. I have a friend who is on an Ayurvedic diet and feels a thousand percent better. She is single with no kids, however, and has time (and more serious health concerns) to manage that. The bottom line is that you do what you can to make more healthy choices when it comes to eating. A donut and a cup of coffee is not a well-balanced breakfast. Contrary to popular belief, the four basic food groups are not chocolate, ice cream, cake, and cola (although I'm pretty sure bacon is its own food group). Maintain a balance of whole grains, proteins, fats, and carbohydrates at every meal. Eat fresh fruits and vegetables whenever possible. Regardless of how you may feel about organics and all that, the balance will help you achieve consistent blood sugar levels. This will help reduce big mood swings and make you feel more in control. Cut down on simple carbs, such as pasta and white bread, and processed sugar (e.g., soda) and caffeine, and eat more colorful foods like sweet potatoes, carrots, and leafy greens. By all means, eat a good balanced breakfast. This will start your day right, making you more alert and clear-thinking, as well as help you avoid snacking on bad things all day. In the long run, it will also help you achieve and maintain a more healthy weight if you, like most people, need to shed a few pounds.

I can't say enough about the value of healthy eating. Try it for a few weeks and you will be amazed at the difference it will make in how you feel, both physically and emotionally.

Water — Drink lots of water. It's good for you. Spring water is my preference, although filtered water is what I mostly drink. It's cheaper, and you don't have all those throw-away plastic bottles. As part of your overall good health, it's important to stay hydrated. Your body is made up of about 60 percent water, so it needs constant replenishment. Your brain and your heart are about 73 percent water. Water helps you feel less hungry and more alert and energetic. Staying hydrated also helps keep our skin healthy, which translates to looking younger. At this challenging point in our lives, we can use a leg up wherever we can get one.

Touch – Physical touch is something we all need. Chances are there hasn't been a lot of good touching going on with you and your husband. A heartfelt hug is worth a thousand words. Seek out touch with the people in your life. Your children (regardless of their age) need hugs. Some people are big huggers and some, as you probably know, are not. With these guys, maybe just a fist bump will do, but try to connect on a physical level with those who are receptive to it. At the very least, embrace your dog, cat, hamster (carefully), ferret, or whatever soft and cuddly creature you have available. It's all about the connection.

Yoga – Yoga is a great way to balance mind, body, and spirit. It is a terrific stress reliever to work out those kinks and blocks we all hold in our bodies. If you have never tried it, I highly recommend it. Not all yoga is created equal. There are many different types to choose from. Hatha yoga is very popular in the United States, and it has several different "branches," so there's something for everyone. Iyengar yoga is physically demanding, with very precise posture. With Astanga vinyasa yoga, the postures are linked to create a flow, also more physically demanding. Sivananda Yoga and Kundalini both incorporate a more spiritual component, with chanting, meditation, and different breathing techniques. If you are generally more athletic and think yoga is too wimpy, try Bikram Yoga (or hot yoga). This is a hearty workout in a heated room, with lots of sweating and sometimes, unfortunately, some tossing of cookies (complete digestion is recommended before class). Restorative Yoga is wonderful—it involves a lot of lying down and very slow stretches. Yoga is literally for EVERYONE: old, young, fit, out of shape, skinny, fat, healthy, injured, active, lazy, etc. You can find independent yoga studios just about anywhere, and most gyms that have classes will have yoga as well. If you are in a very rural area, there's always a choice of DVDs and YouTube. It never hurts to try new things. Expand your "feel-good" resources.

Journal — Some people really like to write (I do! I do!), and some people do not. For those who are open to it, I highly recommend keeping a journal. Writing can be very cathartic. It's even better than talking to yourself and makes you look smarter if you do those things in public (I do both). When you write in a journal, answers will sometimes come to you as you are writing, even if it's about something else entirely. The more you let your subconscious do the writing, the more this will happen. Instead of "Dear Diary, Today I did blah blah blah," try asking yourself some serious questions. It may not be comfortable for everyone, at least not at first, but personally I find it to be extremely revealing. Give it a try—you might be surprised.

Exercise — You may not want to do much of anything right now, but do not abandon your exercise routine during this trying time. If you didn't already have an exercise routine, this is an excellent time to put one in place. As hard as it may be to get motivated, exercise is guaranteed to make you feel better. It goes along with sleeping and eating, however. It is a three-legged stool. The more regular you are about all three, the easier all three will be. If going to a gym seems daunting, just try walking or dust off that bike in the garage. Start slowly and go a block. The next day, go a little faster and a little farther. You get the drift. If you have a dog, there is another reason to go for a walk. If you can't or don't want to go outside, put on some lively music and dance in your living room. The combination of music and movement will lift your spirits. There are many excellent CDs and DVDs to exercise by. Try Pilates or belly dance or aerobics or yoga flow. I did not take my own advice very well on this at first. Then I started doing yoga on my own and then martial arts with my younger son and I loved it! This is a great opportunity to try something new. There must be some physical adventure you have always wanted to embark upon but didn't. Salsa Dancing, scuba diving, fencing? Whatever it is—JUST DO IT!

Disclaimer: Before trying any new physical activity, consult your health professional.

Meditate – I can't say enough about the positive effects of meditation. When you take the time to sit still, be quiet, and open your mind, you will gain peace and clarity. It is a mental, physical, and emotional break that reduces stress and anxiety and gives you a greater sense of calm and self-control. It may be difficult at first to sit still and clear your thoughts. Keep practicing, and it will get easier. I found that it helps to play some music during meditation. You may not have any good meditation music in your CD collection, but don't worry. That's what YouTube is for. There are plenty of selections to choose from that will be for your desired length of time that can help get you in the right frame of mind to meditate. If a meditation practice sounds daunting to you, I encourage you to start with the visualizations at the end of each chapter. If you simply take a few minutes at a time, you will see it gets easier and more relaxing.

Laughter – Do this as much as possible. It has a wonderful physical effect on your body as well as emotional well-being.

There is science behind this. Laughter releases endorphins, your body's natural feel-good chemicals that promote a feeling of well-being and temporarily relieve physical pain. Laughing strengthens your immune system, boosts your energy level, and makes you more mentally alert. It reduces stress and improves the function of blood vessels and increases blood flow. How can you argue with all of that? We are all born with the gift of laughter. Throughout our childhood we have to learn to be serious. You've got to let that go, get back to your roots, and just laugh.

Here are some suggestions: Rent a funny movie. Go to a funny movie. Sometimes the key is the stupider the better. Go to a comedy club with friends. Watch the comedy channel on TV. Go to the animal shelter and play with some puppies or kittens. Read a funny book or get one on tape to listen to in your car. Watch stupid cat videos on YouTube. Hang out with friends who make you laugh. Find more friends who make you laugh. Listen to jokes and then repeat them to give the gift of laughter to other people (make sure you get the punchline right). Laughter truly is the best medicine.

It's easy when we are in pain to lose sight of our sense of humor. If you never actually had one of those, there's no time like the present to get one. When we are surrounded by loss and sadness, we take ourselves and our life entirely too seriously. We look at ourselves pathetically, thinking that this is the worst thing that ever happened to anyone anywhere. That's just not so. Go out and talk to people and you will find that someone out there had a meaner husband, one who cheated more, or was an alcoholic or drug addict, who was abusive, narcissistic, hateful, demeaning, and lazy. And then some people have it really bad. They have lost children, lovers, parents, siblings, their home, their health, body parts, etc. If you actually fit into all of these categories, then God bless you—you do have it bad. As for the rest of us, things could be worse—a lot worse. You may not be able to find the humor in your present separation experience, but there is more going on in your life that you can laugh about. Seek out these things and look on the lighter side. It will help you take a step back and realize that maybe this isn't *so* bad.

There are many ways to achieve, or at least move toward, balance. If you are off balance, everything you try to do will be much more difficult. First and foremost, you must eat properly, get an adequate amount of sleep, and get some form of physical exercise. After that, the best way I have found for most people to regain their balance is with meditation and yoga. Meditation brings calm and clarity, while yoga merges mind, body, and spirit. Another method I have used to restore balance is acupuncture. It is incredibly relaxing and leaves one with a sense of calm and general well-being. People have different opinions and experiences when it comes to the choice of health care professionals. I have tried many alternatives, including chiropractic, acupuncture, foot reflexology, neuro feedback, energy healing, reiki, and regression therapy. I have found benefits in all of these. You should do what works best for you, but I encourage you to have an open mind. Ask people you know for recommendations. And don't forget to laugh.

Exercises

1. Make a shopping list of healthy items so that you can begin eating properly. Go to the store and get them.
2. If you are not sleeping, try the natural methods I suggested before resorting to pharmaceutical assistance.
3. List three things you can do today for exercise. Pick one and do it today.

Visualization

Sit in a quiet place. Get comfortable. Take a deep breath in through your nose and blow it out very slowly through your mouth. With each breath you let out, imagine a part of your body completely relaxing. Start with your head. When you exhale, feel the tension leaving your head. Next, focus on your neck as you exhale. With each breath, move down your body until you get all the way to your toes. Continue to follow your breath as you imagine yourself in a green meadow with wildflowers. You are walking slowly through the meadow, enjoying the warm sun on your face and the gentle breeze in your hair. You feel light and carefree as you find a soft place in the grass to lie down on your back. You are looking at the deep blue sky and the clouds. You feel peaceful and content. You have no cares, no worries. You only have this moment. Close your eyes and stay in that space for a few moments. When you open your eyes again, you will feel more centered.

SECTION II

During the Divorce

TORN

Chapter Five
Professional Help

> "I have learned that not diamonds but divorce lawyers are a girl's best friend."
> — Zsa Zsa Gabor

Even if you and your husband are communicating in a spirit of cooperation and working out details all on your own, I advise getting some professional help. This can come in the form of child specialists, therapists, mediators, financial planners, business valuators, and, of course, lawyers. The most expensive of these professionals is going to be the lawyer. Depending on where you live, these cost anywhere from $250 per hour (small town, inexperienced) all the way up to $1000 per hour for experienced, big city types. Ouch. Now imagine every conversation you and your husband have has to go through these. That's per hour times two. Ouch! Other professionals can help you work out your differences at less than half the rate *before* you take it to these high priced attorneys for the final legal decree.

My Story — I have a good friend who is an attorney, so as soon as my husband dropped his big news, I asked her for a recommendation. Even though I was in denial and trying to get him to stay those first few weeks, enough of me was rooted in reality to start preparing for the inevitable. I didn't have any idea what kind of attorney to get, or what the different divorce options might be. My friend gave me several names, and I found one I liked who was trained in collaborative, or cooperative, divorce. That sounded good to me, as I wanted to avoid an all-out war that some other attorneys specialize in. My husband had already seen an attorney before he even told me his plans. His recommendation came from our business attorney, Paul, who sent him to one of those war kind of attorneys. We'll call that guy Richard. Richard told my husband, among other things, that he would pay me child support, but I would just spend it on myself and then constantly be hitting him up for money. Oh, thanks for that recommendation, Paul. My attorney knew Richard and told me she wouldn't work with him. I told my husband that, and he actually changed attorneys—twice—until we were on the same page. He was feeling a little guilty, so also accommodating, but I think mostly he knew the war would be too expensive and take too long. My husband and I actually worked out most of the details of the decree as far as division of assets and custody issues. We sat with our attorneys on several occasions to work through the language and some things we hadn't even thought of. Because we shared a business, we also both had to consult business attorneys. He used our business attorney, Paul. I think there must be some kind of unethical conflict of interest there, but that's water under the bridge. It never occurred to me to consult a financial planner to advise me of my financial options, with the pros and cons of each. I thought we could figure it out and the lawyers would help. I don't feel like I got ripped off, but I also don't feel like I had all the information I should have had to make the right choices. We also did not have our business valued. We had had a valuation done a couple of years prior, so we just went with that. My husband was extremely motivated to get the divorce over with so he could move on with his life, guilt-free. He rushed the divorce through in record time. Divorces on average take 12 to 18 months from filing to finalization. Ours took a short 83 days. I'm glad it was not painfully drawn out, but I made decisions affecting the rest of my life without being fully prepared because I let him intimidate me. If I had taken more time, I believe I would have made different decisions, but again, water under the bridge. We had enough assets that I was far from being on the street, but to this day I have some legal ties that I would rather not have. My divorce attorney tried to tell me a thing or two that I now wish I had listened to.

Collaborative vs. Cooperative – I mentioned both a collaborative and a cooperative divorce. A collaborative divorce involves multiple people, which could include a child specialist, financial planner, mediator, etc. While these people are all helpful to the process, remember that they each come with their own separate hourly rates, which definitely add up, especially if everyone is in the room at the same time. Engaging the services of less expensive professionals to work out the details prior to drafting the decree will reduce the overall costs of the divorce, as I'll detail below. By contrast, a cooperative divorce is one in which you and your spouse sit down with your lawyers and make decisions that go into the decree. If you have the ability to work out some details on your own without the lawyers, then that will obviously save you some time and money. This is the route my ex-husband and I took. We hashed out a lot beforehand, and sometimes in meetings with our lawyers, ironically, my ex-husband and I teamed up against them. We did this because we

thought we knew more than them. In some cases we did, but mostly not.

Financial Planner – There are two points that take up the vast majority of negotiating time and legal paper. Those are the children and the money. Let's start with the money. In the chaotic mass of betrayal, infidelity, lost dreams, disappointments, and anger, there is no catalyst for upheaval as effective as the discussion of money. As one of the top three things couples fight about, chances are it has been a point of contention at some point in your relationship already. It is easy to lose sight of the big picture when the discussion comes down to money. Working with a financial planner—one who has CDFA (Certified Divorce Financial Advisor) after his or her name—will help navigate this issue, and if done before meeting with the lawyers, will save you hundreds, if not thousands, of dollars. This person will sit down with you and run numbers for every possible scenario. If you are attached to keeping the house, they can show you the pros and cons of that. Should you take 401k money or the lake house? Are you going to be better off with cash or the stock fund? You can work with this person on your own, or you and your husband can work together with them to come to an equitable solution.

Some people want to get divorced, but stay together because "they can't afford it." What that really means is they can't afford to maintain their current lifestyle times two households. It also probably means they are not really sure they want to get a divorce. If you're satisfied staying in the same house for financial convenience, that's up to you, but it will be very difficult for you (or him) to move on with your lives. If there is that other woman that he is seeing, staying in the same house, regardless of how far apart your separate bedrooms are, is a recipe for disaster. I have never seen that go well. A good financial planner can also help you figure out how to make the transition to two households.

Before you meet with a financial planner, put together a comprehensive list of all of your assets. If you, like many women, especially those who have been married a very long time, don't know what or where all of your financial assets are, get that list from your husband. If he hesitates, point out that he is legally required to provide it. If the asset list is complex, or if your husband is not forthcoming with the list, or if you suspect he is leaving something out, your financial planner may recommend the services of a forensic accountant. A forensic accountant will comb through all of your financial records to ensure that nothing is left out. These are the same people who go over the records of a business to uncover embezzlement and fraud. On the flip side of that, if you have been socking away money, it is best to be upfront about it.

If you and your husband have a prenuptial agreement in place, you will need to show this to your financial advisor. Be advised that they generally hold up pretty well. See more about that later in this chapter.

Child Specialist – The child specialist is a mental health professional with expertise in children's developmental needs. This person is a neutral consultant who meets with the parents to determine what their goals are in regard to the children. They will ask about any concerns or fears either parent has about custody, access, living arrangements, and repercussions from the divorce for the children, etc. They can help determine how and when to tell the children about the upcoming separation.

The child specialist can then also meet alone with the children to talk to them about the upcoming changes and determine how the children might respond and what their resulting needs are. The child specialist can help the parents work out a parenting plan that best meets their goals, while taking into account the children's perspectives. The parents then have a sustainable plan that works for the whole family to give to the attorneys to write into the divorce decree.

Mediator — A mediator is trained and experienced in dispute resolution. They are neutral facilitators who sit down with both you and your husband to help you work out all of the negotiating points of your divorce, from asset division to child custody to retirement and tax issues. The mediator does not judge who is right or wrong and does not give legal advice.

As with the financial professional, a mediator is much less expensive than an attorney. Using a mediator instead of your attorneys to facilitate your agreement will save you a lot of money. It is the mediator's job to keep the peace when things get heated and to keep you on track when communication breaks down. It may be necessary to have several sessions with the mediator to come to full agreement.

In order for mediation to be effective, both parties have to be willing to make some concessions and abide by the mediation. As the mediator is neutral and unbiased, they don't represent either party. They, therefore, do not take the place of an attorney or a financial planner. Your attorney and your financial planner are advocates for you—to get what is best for you, while still being fair. While you may reach agreement in mediation, your attorney or financial planner may point out something there that is not in your best interest. In this case you may need to go back to the mediator.

Regardless of which professionals you engage, all of the sessions are private. Anything you can do to keep your divorce out of court is a good thing. The divorce court is public. Anyone can sit in court and hear the specifics. Unlike the use of the above mentioned professionals, a divorce in the court system will limit communication and put the decisions about your and your children's futures in the hands of a stranger.

Lawyer – If you are still in the beginning stages of your divorce, or if you are planning one, you will at some point need to engage the services of an attorney. You and your husband cannot share one, no matter how amicable you think this may be. There is an abundance of jokes about bad lawyers, but there are also many, many good lawyers out there. Find a good one. When I say that, I do not mean go out and find one that will fight dirty to get you everything and leave your spouse in the dust. That is not a good one. That is a bad one. Many women, in the heat of the moment of feeling scorned will say something like "I'm going to take you for everything you have!" The temptation, then, would be to engage the services of one of those "war" attorneys. This kind of lawyer can do far more damage to your ongoing relationship, your feelings of self-worth, and your children's welfare than the worst of your marriage did. And remember, the more money you give to lawyers, the less money is available to split. While you certainly have a right to be angry at this point, a war will have untold costs beyond just the money. A good lawyer is one who has been trained in "collaborative" or "cooperative" divorce. He or she is one who will work with your partner's lawyer to come to a fair and equitable solution. This is a lawyer who will keep you out of court and end up saving you thousands of dollars. Obviously this will work much better if your spouse will do the same. If you have been doing this whole thing gracefully up until now, perhaps he will be more receptive to the idea of a cooperative divorce, especially when you point out the cost savings. If you or your husband were unfaithful, it will not make that big of a difference to a judge. The attitude about that will differ depending on the laws of your state. Their first concern is the children and after that dividing assets equally. These days, infidelity is so commonplace that it is no longer much of a consideration anymore, unless the children are directly adversely affected by it. How you and your lawyer handle this stage of the breakup will make a major difference in the climate of your relationship with your spouse from this point forward.

If you are thinking that you and your spouse can just hash this out without a lawyer to save a few bucks, I would advise you to reconsider. A divorce decree is a legal document, and you need a law professional to help you negotiate it. I applaud you for trying to keep everything fair and friendly. You can still do that, but it is my opinion that you each need your own attorney. Yes, it is expensive. Perhaps it seems like a waste of money because you trust your spouse, and, like you, he only wants what's fair. I'm sorry to tell you that you may be in for a bit of a shock. It may not even come up for several years down the road. You don't know how you will feel about each other a year from now or two years from now, or what other influencers may come in to play.

One more thing about divorce lawyers is that they have seen a lot of divorces. They know how these things go and what inevitably happens in the end. Listen to what they tell you. You have the option to go against their advice, but at least you will be making an informed decision.

Online Divorce – There are some alternatives. If your divorce is very simple (no kids, no business, and no property) and you really have worked out all the details, check out online services. Google online divorce, and all kinds of things come up. If you choose to go this route, do your homework. Be aware that not everything on the internet that seems like a good deal is actually a good deal. There are scammers everywhere, other fees get added, and you may end up in court anyway. If that happens, the internet service will not be there to represent you. One service I have seen recommended, although I have no personal experience with them, is Wevorce.com.

Pre-Nuptial Agreements – Rules for prenups vary from state to state, and each contract has to be evaluated on its individual merits. If you want your lawyer to help you get out of your prenup, he or she will look to see which of the rules may have been broken when the contract was signed. There are three main questions they will ask: When was it signed? Where was it signed? Under what conditions was it signed? The closer to the wedding it was signed, the more likely it could be thrown out. This has to do with there not being ample time to fully understand the contents. If your husband gave you the prenup the day before the wedding and you signed it without the benefit of legal counsel, you may have a case for breaking the contract. Unless specifically addressed in the prenup, infidelity will not render the agreement invalid. If you signed it in good faith, with

legal counsel, and not under duress, then it will most likely stand. Every marriage and subsequent divorce is different, and only you know your exact situation. I only suggest, in the spirit of what's fair, you be honest about why you might want to break it.

Negotiation and Compromise – Pretty much everything is negotiable. When your decree is being written, you don't have to stay with all the standard language. If you want to change up the standard every-other-weekend-and-Wednesday-evening thing for the non-custodial parent, then do what makes sense for your situation. Maybe one week at a time would work better for you. Hopefully this is something you and your partner can agree upon before the lawyers are involved. If this is a sticking point, the child specialist should be able to help. If you have a situation where it is just not possible for the two of you to speak, then your lawyers can hash it out, but remember they do work for you and should respect what you want. I will, however, repeat what I said about lawyers knowing more about divorce than you do. Yes, your situation is unique, but they have the numbers on their side. If they are adamantly resisting some changes you want to make, at least listen to why.

Like in any successful marriage, there is an abundance of compromise in a successful divorce. "He's not gonna tell *me...*" and "the day she gets *that...*" are not statements of compromise. I know, you already feel like you have given up everything. Maybe just walking away is the compromise—accepting what IS and moving on. Getting to what's fair is what is important. Think about what is really crucial and choose your battles around those things. Just about everything else can be negotiated for a win-win compromise. If the word "compromise" bothers you and seems like something that involves losing ground by splitting the difference, try "cooperative problem solving." This is a more creative approach that brings a solution to meet everyone's needs.

Decree – This document, like all legal documents, is written by and for lawyers. It is long and complex. You must read and understand every word. If you do not understand any part of it, have your lawyer explain it to you. That's what you pay them for. This document will affect you for the rest of your life, so indulge me as I repeat myself. Read and understand every part of your divorce decree *before* you sign it. If you have children, the bulk of the decree will be about them. Details about custody, child support, holidays, and time with the non-custodial parent are all spelled out. Make sure it is written the way you and your partner have agreed. It may seem like you don't need all these minute details, but they are there for a reason (besides just billable hours for your attorney).

There are some common optional additions to your decree. One of these is called the paramour clause. The purpose of this clause is to help your children during the adjustment period by limiting their exposure to mom's or dad's new romantic interest. The language varies depending on what the two of you agree upon. Mine just stated that neither of us were allowed to introduce a new romantic partner for a specified period of time. Many of these clauses are very restrictive, in effect as long as the children are minors, but may involve only sleepovers. I am a fan of this clause. It's hard enough for your children to process the fact that the two of you are no longer a couple, without bringing in the replacements. If this new person is important, then it won't hurt to wait a little while to set up housekeeping until the children have some time to adjust. Respect it and adhere to it. It is there for a good reason.

Another optional clause has to do with money. To discourage one party from accidentally leaving some assets off of the list, this clause states that any money that is discovered after the decree is finalized will be given exclusively to the other party. Inclusion of this wording has led to more than one sudden recall. "Oh, yeah, there's this other account I forgot all about."

There can also be restrictions about where the custodial parent can live. My decree stated that I could not move outside of a two-county area. That sounds restrictive, but we agreed to keep our boys in the same school district and those two counties were quite large. It was also much more convenient for everyone that our households were just several miles apart. This is another important point to work out if possible prior to involving the lawyers.

Even in the most amicable of splits, there is plenty of room for misunderstandings and failed memories. This document will stand as the fallback in case there is a dispute. That doesn't mean every detail in the decree has to be followed to the letter all the time. You and your ex can switch days and holidays and pick up times as long as you both agree (I recommend doing this in writing and keeping copies just in case). In the absence of said agreement, your divorce decree will come in very handy. I used it more than once as a tool to stand up for my rights.

Fairness – I talk a lot about accepting responsibility, letting go, and doing the right thing. This is in no way meant to say just roll over and take what is shoveled your way. In a perfect world, everything written in this book would go both ways. You stand up and hold your head high and conduct yourself with dignity and grace. Most of the time, this conduct will be met in kind. If you smile directly at someone, it is unusual if they don't smile back, even if just a little corner of the mouth moves. If you make a concerted effort to be fair, your partner most likely will as well. If your husband has been cheating, or otherwise recognizes he treated you poorly, he is more likely to want to be fair now. However, if he is leaving you because he's angry about something you did, or something he thinks you did, he may refuse to play along nicely, and you will need to stand up for yourself. If he gets a nasty attorney and insists on going to court, you will need to find an attorney that has experience in that kind of divorce. Fair goes both ways, so you need to be fair to yourself as well as to your former partner. This is a very difficult and stressful time under the best circumstances. If this person is intent on fighting and being nasty, that makes the advice in this book a much bigger challenge. Do not let yourself sink to the lowest common denominator. Appreciate the challenge, and if you have to fight to get what you are entitled to, then by all means fight, but fight fair.

An unfortunate side effect of divorce is, of course, the cost. It won't be free, and the more you have to hash out and divide up, the more it is going to cost. Being civil to one another and communicating directly is the best way to save money. Bring in the professionals you need to advise you and save the lawyers for the strictly legal questions. To the degree possible, leave them out of the back and forth negotiations, as they are two to five times the cost of the other professionals I have listed.

Exercises

1. Make a list of all of your assets. Don't forget things like 401ks, investments, and insurance policies
2. Make a list of things you want included in your divorce decree. Put a "D" next to the items that are desirable but negotiable. Put an "N" next to items that are non-negotiable.
3. If you haven't done so already, do some research to find a financial planner and a lawyer. Make sure these individuals specialize in divorce.

Visualization

Sit in a quiet place. Get comfortable. Take a deep breath in through your nose and blow it out very slowly through your mouth. With each breath you let out, imagine a part of your body completely relaxing. Start with your head. When you exhale, feel the tension leaving your head. Next, focus on your neck as you exhale. With each breath, move down your body until you get all the way to your toes. Continue to follow your breath as you imagine you are walking along a beach. Feel the breeze in your hair. Notice the scent of salt in the air. Hear the rhythmic sound of the waves. You feel completely at peace and you continue to relax. Notice the shells on the beach. A crab scurries into a hole he makes in the sand. You hear the cry of a seagull. Everything is calm. Everything is as it should be in this moment. Stay with this vision until you feel it. Everything is okay.

Chapter Six
The Kids

"The best security blanket a child can have is
parents who respect each other"
— Jane Blaustone

What is the point of a graceful ending? For the most part, it is for our own dignity and self-respect. For me, the most important reason for all the frustration of trying to "be the bigger person" was my children. They are not to blame for the problems in our marriages. They have no control over our fighting, our refusal to listen, our inability to compromise, our failure to be the person our spouse wants us to be, or the lying and cheating that goes on way too often. Children bear the brunt of divorce long after the parents have moved on. They are the ones who have to shuttle between houses. They are the ones who have to tiptoe around hurt feelings and backbiting exes. When they have families of their own, they may have FOUR sets of in-laws to keep happy on the holidays. The very least we owe our children is to be civil to their other parent, no matter what injustice we feel we have suffered at their hand. We can sit together at events so our kids don't have to choose between us—even in that very small way. We can be in the same wedding pictures with them.

Rebecca Donovan

We can tolerate the new wife—yes, even if that new wife is THE OTHER WOMAN—and be civil to her as well.

My Story — When we told our children that we were going to get divorced, it was the most difficult conversation of my life. It will forever be etched in my memory, and thinking about it could bring tears to my eyes for some time afterward. We had talked with a child specialist for advice, and, of course, I had read several books on the subject as well as scouring the internet. I was very nervous, and actually had some stuff written out. We agreed ahead of time to leave out the ugly details of the breakup and tell them it was a mutual decision. I believed at the time and still believe today that it was in their best interest to have a solid relationship with both parents and that they should not be burdened with matters they had no control over and didn't understand. If you talk to 20 people on this subject, they will have 20 different opinions about it. This is what we felt was the best thing for our children.

Just as I had initially believed that the changes to my life would be intolerable, I also thought my children would be irreparably harmed by the divorce. Without a doubt, there were consequences for the children, but I didn't give mine enough credit. We had travelled extensively with them and had exposed them to a lot of different people, places, and circumstances. We had raised them thus far to be resilient and flexible, and they were. Of course, when we told them we were getting divorced, they were sad, mostly, I think, because they thought they should be.

When it came time for Brian to move out, we all participated in the move. He left a lot of our belongings but took quite a few with him for continuity. I helped him set up his kitchen in the new apartment and helped the boys with their room. I was still sad about the breakup, but by the time he actually moved out it had been over two months, and I was starting to see some positive sides to the whole thing. In those first months before he was allowed to introduce his girlfriend to them, we were still a family. We just had two households. I had a key to the apartment, so if anything got left behind it was no big deal. The kids were fine and it looked like it would be as successful as these things can be. Once the girlfriend entered as a permanent addition, things went downhill, but I'll talk more about that later.

Doing the move the way we did was the best thing for our kids. It was difficult for me to go about my business like nothing was wrong before telling them, but I wanted to wait because they were at the end of the school year and I was worried it would have a negative impact on their school work. There was no big, mysterious "Where did Daddy go?" My emotions were much more in control at that point, so the move itself was not as difficult for me as it would have been if it had happened sooner. Brian had already filed for divorce, so there was no leftover denial. The apartment came with a pool, so that was a plus, and they spent a lot of time at dad's playing video games together. They enjoyed being there with him because his time with them was dedicated to them. That would eventually change, but that summer was actually pretty good for them.

What to Tell Your Kids — Like I said, the way we handled the announcement and subsequent move was the best thing for our family. You will have to decide what is best for yours. A quick trip to the internet and Amazon.com will show you the vast array of books and articles available on this subject. The most important question to ask yourself when deciding how to tell your children is this: What will make this transition easiest for the children? Try to tell them some semblance of the truth without going into the minutia surrounding the facts. An all-out lie will probably come back to bite you later. You may have to check your pride at the door and suck it up on the humility, but these are the most important people in the world and you want to help them through this life altering upheaval. Don't try to make them help **you** through it. I have two very adaptable boys, and the way we handled the transition to two households worked well for all of us. There is no perfect way to handle it because it is such an imperfect situation, but think it through and try to see it from their point of view. Always remember, they love you **both. Do not ever** try to make them choose between you. If they decide on their own to take sides, do not encourage them. Let them talk through their feelings and express their anger, disappointment, etc. Listen, but don't egg them on. It isn't a contest, and unless the other parent is a danger to them, it isn't healthy for them to think they hate one of you. I have found that taking sides is much more prevalent among adult children in their 20s. They think they have it all figured out, and it makes them angry to see evidence to the contrary. They want things to be black and white, so they need to make one parent all good and the other all bad. The most you can do is to be as truthful as possible, patient, and kind. Some family therapy can be very helpful if they'll go. Otherwise, time, experience, and maturity should eventually prevail.

There are many ways to diverge households. For the majority of families, the dad moves to an apartment or in with a friend or family member. Maybe it would be better for your situation for you to move out. This may seem counterintuitive at first, but don't discount the possibility. You may want to get a place that's closer to work or near friends. You may want to stay with a friend or family for emotional support. If you stay in the house, you will be responsible for all of the maintenance of the house, which can add considerable stress to your life. There can be a great deal of freedom in renting, even temporarily. When you move out, you can take what you need and leave him to deal with the rest of it.

Another of these options is something a good friend of mine and her husband decided to do. The kids stayed in the house and the parents took turns being there. When it was his turn with the kids, she stayed with her mom, and when it was hers, he stayed with his brother. This option probably works better when there are no third parties involved. In the situation where there is that other woman, he might want to stay at her place when he's not with the kids. If it's too soon for you, this may not be the best option, but remember you cannot control what he does when he's not with the kids.

The standard time split is a night or two per week for dad plus every other weekend and then some set time in the summer. Some people still do that, but it's not always practical. We pretty much divided time equally, as we never lived that far apart, so getting them to and from school wasn't a big deal. Some people do alternate weeks. Others do weekdays/weekends. How you choose to do the multiple household thing all depends on your individual situation, but understand there are always alternative options. You can try different schedules to see what works. Whatever you choose, however, try to factor in what makes it easiest for the kids and give them the schedule so they always know where they're going to be and when. It's annoying for them to think they'll be one place and make plans with their friends and then find out they are somewhere else. Remember, this is stressful for them, too.

Parenting – You owe it to your children to be the best parent you can be. Sometimes the decision to divorce is about just that. If you and your spouse make each other crazy, it is hard to focus on your children. Don't get me wrong. I don't advocate getting divorced as a general parenting improvement plan, but if you are horribly, irrevocably unhappy in your marriage, you cannot possibly focus on your children to the extent you should. In the perfect world, children have two parents who love each other and live together in the family unit as partners in parenting. In the absence of said perfect world, however, it is possible to be parenting partners and do a good job as divorced parents. The first step, of course, is to rise above your differences and put your children where they belong—at the top of your priority list. Try to reach agreement on presenting a consistent rule base at each of your respective homes. Things like homework expectations, video game and television time, along with bedtimes and required chores should be as similar as is reasonable. This consistency helps the children know what to expect. It also avoids the "easy house/ hard house" classifications, which can lead to the children trying to play each parent against the other. Initially, when it's just you at your house and your soon-to-be-ex-husband at the other house, this shouldn't be too hard unless you always had drastically different parenting styles. I will talk more later about what happens when the girlfriend moves in with them. For now, before that happens, it's good to establish some good habits that work. The best way to make that happen is for the two of you to be openly communicating with each other. If that's not possible at this point, I would suggest using some sort of mediation, which, as we've discussed, is far less expensive than running everything through your lawyers.

If you suspect abuse or neglect at the other house, that is another matter altogether and requires immediate action on your part. It is always your responsibility to protect your children. Be absolutely certain you have your facts straight before making any accusations, and above all, make sure you act in the best interest of your children and not out of vengeance or other self-serving motives.

If your kids are with you the majority of the time, do your best to involve their father in important aspects of their lives, even when they occur on your time. If he is more or less absent, continue to inform him of things like soccer games and band concerts and teacher meetings. It will mean something to your kids if/when he shows up.

Bad-mouthing – So, you want the world to know how much you have been injured and just exactly what that so-and-so did to you. He never was that good in bed, spent money recklessly, had body odor, drank excessively, cheated, got fat, etc. Not only do most people not **need** to know this stuff, they **really don't want** to know it. It will leave you in a bad light and have people wondering if maybe there was a good reason why that person is not with you anymore. Never bad-mouth your ex to the children you share. It only hurts the children. In addition, do not, under any circumstances, allow your current boyfriend/girlfriend, friends, or family to bad-mouth your children's other parent in front of the child. Continuation of this behavior should be grounds for dismissal of that particular relationship. Your relationship with your children is the MOST IMPORTANT one that you have.

When you tell a child that his or her other parent is bad, it is like ripping off a piece of the child's very essence and stomping on it.

Children perceive themselves as part of each of you. You cannot put down the other parent without putting down the child. Never use your children to "get" the other parent. It only hurts the child, and they have already been hurt enough. Bad-mouthing the new girlfriend is an extension of bad-mouthing the father. Don't do it. It will only confuse, anger, and hurt your child for you to do so.

One more thing about taking care of your children. When I say your relationship with your children is the most important one you have, I mean the most important one you have with someone else. Your relationship with yourself is the most important relationship you have. There is a reason why the flight attendant tells us to put our oxygen mask on before helping others. If you are not breathing, you are no help to anyone. You must take care of yourself before you can do your kids any good.

When my divorce was pending, I read a lot of statistics about the effects of divorce on children. Pre-teen boys, they say, tend to take it the hardest. My boys were nine and twelve when we separated. They were affected, certainly, but they came out okay. Since you can't go back and see what would have happened if the divorce didn't occur, you can't know for sure what was caused by the divorce and what was just life playing itself out. I do know that how you handle the initial separation, the divorce itself, and all the communication in the years to follow will have much further reaching consequences than the fact that there was a divorce. You owe it to your children to do your part to make a smooth transition.

Exercises

1. If you haven't told your children yet about the divorce, write out some things you want to say. Discuss this with your husband, if possible. The more you are on the same page, the better.
2. Imagine you are your children. What would be your biggest concern upon hearing that your parents are separating?
3. Make some time this week to do something special with your kids. Make the activity only about them.

Visualization

Sit in a quiet place. Get comfortable. Take a deep breath in through your nose and blow it out very slowly through your mouth. With each breath you let out, imagine a part of your body completely relaxing. Start with your head. When you exhale, feel the tension leaving your head. Next, focus on your neck as you exhale. With each breath, move down your body until you get all the way to your toes. Continue to follow your breath as you imagine you are in a garden. You are walking along a path lined with beautiful flowers. Bend down to gather their aroma. At the end of the path, you come to a large fountain that has a bright light emanating from it. Hold your arms wide and imagine the light wrapping around you and filling your body. Now close your eyes and imagine your children encircled in that same light with you. Hold them in a close embrace as you are filled with the love you feel for them. Stay in this space for a few moments. Open your eyes as you hold on to that warm feeling.

Rebecca Donovan

At your first opportunity, go tell your children that you love them and wrap them in a big hug.

Chapter Seven

Communication

"First learn the meaning of what
you say, and then speak."
— Epictetus

The way you communicate with your husband during this divorce process will set the tone for your relationship going forward. He may be taking your wrath right now because he's feeling guilty about how things went down. This, in all likelihood, will be short-lived. The nastier you are to him now, the less guilty he will feel and the more he will fight you at every turn. You can weigh the pros and cons of continuing to have a relationship with him from a number of different perspectives. First and foremost, if you have children with this man, it is in everyone's best interest (including yours) to have an amicable relationship with him. If there are no children and you have no plans to ever see or speak to him again, there are a still couple of reasons to be civil. As I said above, the meaner you are to him, the meaner he will be in return to you. This will cost you money. The more you fight, the more the lawyers get. The pettier you are, the pettier he will be. Items that mean something to you will become items he fights for. On the other hand, items you could really do without, but fought for out of spite, end up in your garage collecting dust. And, don't forget the matter of your self-respect and integrity. He cannot take that from you, but you *can* hand it over. If you allow yourself to be spiteful and bitter during this process, it becomes much more difficult for you to move on because you are just fueling the anger and resentment and hate that will only come back to hurt you. When he is happily setting up housekeeping with his new girlfriend, no amount of seething or tying yourself in knots will affect him. You might as well bang your head on the wall. He won't feel it, but you will have a terrible headache.

My Story — If my husband had just come to me at some point and said, "Hey, this is not working. I want a divorce," of course I would have been sad, but it would have been easier to take. Adding that other person to the mix just made everything ugly. Ironically, between the time Brian told me he was leaving, and when he actually moved out, we communicated more openly and honestly than we did in our entire marriage. Most of the sticking points were about her. HER. She moved to town and didn't have a car, so he let her drive his old car. I said no way, because that was community property. I won that argument. He sold her the car. She wrote him a check for $100, and he gave me half. Yes, I won that argument. I could have pursued the matter, but a wise friend advised me to pick my battles. The car wasn't worth all that much, and in the grand scheme of things it didn't matter. And, as always with Brian, I couldn't outsmart him. He came from a long line of manipulators, and I was not a match. Not even close.

There were some arguments along the way, about stuff and money, and, of course, about her. For the most part, we communicated pretty well. Our divorce cost more than a drop in the bucket since we had a business, kids, and multiple properties, but I shudder to think about the money we could have dropped if we had refused to communicate with each other. We agreed on most things in the decree ahead of time, so we saved there. We had already established the routine for the boys before we talked to lawyers. I could always tell when I was communicating only with him (mostly in emails) and when there had been consultation with her. Yes, I very much resented the fact that not only was she the main cause of the divorce, but was also involved in the negotiations. On the other side of that, he was also involved in her divorce from her husband. I can imagine how that guy must have felt as well.

One thing I did that may or may not be plausible for you, if you are in the same situation, is to meet with "the other woman." I knew she was going to be in my children's lives, probably as their stepmother, and I wanted to meet her before they did. She agreed, but I imagine he had to talk her into it. If I were in her shoes, I would have been terrified. I could have made it very uncomfortable for her, screamed at her and called her a home-wrecking whore. Things I had said in the shower and in my car. But my goal in meeting her was to establish a relationship. "Are you nuts?" you may ask. No. My kids had two parents, and whether I liked it or not, their other parent came with an attachment. I had several divorced friends who had managed to make parenting a team effort with success. I was the only one I knew whose divorce came with a stepmother for my kids, but in the end it was about the kids. So I met her for a glass (or two) of wine. She was nervous, but pleasant. I told her I didn't want to talk about anything that had happened, that I just wanted to start from that day forward. Her sigh of relief was visible. We had an amiable conversation, got to know each other a little bit, and I felt better about her in regard to my kids. She seemed normal.

Rebecca Donovan

She wasn't, and the relationship deteriorated over the years. I'm still baffled by it, but I feel completely confident that I did everything I could to make it work.

Kindness – You have the option in every situation to be kind or unkind. From the grocery store clerk, to the unfriendly postal worker (there I go, stereotyping), to your children and your former partner, if you approach the encounter with kindness, you will be amazed at the results. True, some people will make it difficult to be kind. These are an extra challenge. Appreciate the daily challenges and try the kindness. More often than not, people will react positively to your efforts. Even if they don't show it, they will be, even at some miniscule level, affected by it. What showing kindness will *always* do, however, is make you feel better about yourself. You may have to work up to this in small ways if you are not used to it, but it will become natural. Be the bigger person. Show some kindness.

Honesty – Above all, be honest with yourself. Every morning you have to look at yourself in the mirror. Lying to yourself will get you nowhere. There are certain steps one must take to go through the healing process, and if you are telling yourself one thing and doing another, it's not going to help you. If you have trouble with this issue, sit down with the most brutally honest person you know (and trust) and ask them to lay it out for you. It may not be pretty, but you have to know where you stand with yourself. Once you are being honest with yourself, it will be easier to be honest with others, especially your ex. Honesty does have its limits, of course. Some things are better left unsaid.

Intent – Before making a statement to or about your former spouse, before taking some drastic action, think about your intent. What is the expected outcome of what you are about to say or do? Be honest with yourself, and think about it again. Do you really think that your ex-husband will see his new lover in a different light if you just point out her faults to him? Do you really believe that your kids will love you more if you say something bad about their father? Do you really think your neighbors will like or respect you more if you tell them sordid details of your crumbled marriage? No, no, and no. Revisit your intent. If your true intent is to make someone look bad or feel bad, then don't do it. If your intent is to sabotage someone's job, friendships, or new relationship, stop. If your intent is to make yourself feel better by making another person look bad, think again. This does not work—ever. Rethink your intent.

Integrity – Graceful endings require this in good measure. When you have integrity, it's one of those things that can define your very essence. One that can never be taken from you. You walk with your chin held high and everyone recognizes that you have it. Integrity earns you respect as it travels with you to all of your relationships, be they friendships, romantic involvements, or business affiliations. Best of all is the way it enhances your relationship with yourself. When you have integrity, you can stand in front of the mirror and look yourself right in the eye every morning without faltering.

I was discussing the concept of integrity with a divorced male friend of mine recently and he said I was assuming that both parties in the divorce were rational people who **wanted** to act in a dignified manner. He thought all of this stuff would be irrelevant

Rebecca Donovan

if your pending ex-partner was the devious, crazy person that so many people you talk to seem to be divorced from. Certainly, if both parties were always able to agree to do the breakup with integrity and grace, the divorce courts would be practically empty and there would be more unemployment among divorce attorneys. Some people appear to need drama and angst in their lives and will go to extremes to create it. But you do not have to play along with them. Acting with class will help to diffuse even the most volatile of situations. It is unrealistic to expect any of us to always be a saint and never react to hatefulness, especially when it is hurled directly at us. We can, however, take the time to **think** before we act. Pause just a moment before hitting the send button. There are some people out there who are certifiably insane, and no matter what you do, they will continue to be freaks. We cannot control the actions of another person, but we can control our own. Most people respond favorably to someone who is **genuinely** interested in the win-win.

Obscenities – I have read recently that people who swear are smarter and have a larger vocabulary than people who don't. I didn't make that up. It's science. Who am I to argue with science? That being said, however, while in conversations with your soon-to-be ex, written and verbal, keep it G-rated. No one ever thinks less of you for NOT swearing. If you are ranting and dropping the "F" bomb every other word, you just might find that come up in front of a judge who finds that sort of thing offensive (especially when you are a "girl"—yes, double standards are still alive and well). When you see it in something you've written, you may wish you would have used less colorful language. Although the "F" word can be very versatile—some people use it as a standard adjective, adverb, verb, and noun—when used in anger,

it is quite aggressive. lt rarely takes the conversation where you want it to go if you're aiming for a win-win. The exception here is in that first conversation you had where he told you he was leaving. Whatever language you used in the heat of THAT moment can be excused. We're only human after all.

Along these lines, if you have junk photos of your ex (or really anyone, ever) on your phone or computer, remove them. Just take a moment, put the book down, and go delete them. Call me old fashioned (I've been called worse), but as I've advised my children for years, once something is out there in cyberspace, it's out there. Do you honestly believe the photos sent to and from your phone and computer are private? Really? Do not, under any circumstances, share these photos with anyone. Just delete them.

Perspective – One of my strengths, and one of my weaknesses, is that l can see the big picture most of the time. l look at a situation and usually have the ability to view it from the other person's perspective. l say this is also a weakness because it makes me second guess myself. l find that many people don't have the ability to do this, and furthermore, don't see a need for it. There are absolutely (at least) two sides to every story. l talk to people about their former spouses and am continually amazed at how **bad** those people are. If you look only at the perspective of the person with whom you are talking, there are a whole lot of dangerously psychotic, recently divorced individuals out there. lt's pretty scary. Sometimes you actually then meet those people (or know them already) and say, "What are you talking about? He/she seems pretty normal to me." Sometimes you meet them and say, "Oh, yeah, l see what you mean," but more often than not, the other person is really not as bad as you've been led to believe. The "injured party" has developed this opinion from a series of failed expectations, hurt feelings, and escalating reactions to reactions. It's all a matter of perspective. It will help you understand why your former lover did what he did if you will try to see his point of view. Even in the case of cheating, it can help to try to walk in his shoes for a moment. That is not meant to excuse bad behavior, but just to try to **understand** it. To quote the Bible, "Judge not, lest ye be judged." It's right up there with the Golden Rule. It's hard not to judge just a little, especially if your partner was lying and cheating and stealing your money, but what happened, happened. Your ability to move past it and create your own future and your own happiness can be enhanced by trying to understand the other side of the issue—even just a little.

His perspective – While I do not excuse his methods, I do understand why Brian wanted out of our marriage, at least the way our marriage was at that time. We were both very unhappy. I recently spoke at length with a minister who specializes in counseling men in divorce. The vast majority of counseling and coaching specialties are for women. It's basically a supply and demand issue. Men don't typically ask for help. If you've ever been lost with a man and tried to get him to stop for directions, you know what I mean. I think that is changing a little, and I hope it does because men need help as much as women do. Suicide rates among divorced men are twice as high as those for married men. Conversely, suicide rates aren't any different for married women as they are for divorced women. Why do so many divorced men choose to end their lives? There are a thousand theoretical answers to that question, most of them assigning blame anywhere except on the man who makes that

choice. The women they are divorcing from are evil, the court system is set on destroying men, someone turns their children against them, etc. I don't bring all this up to assign blame or make anyone feel guilty. I bring it up to remind you that while your husband has made the decision to end your marriage, he is still a thinking, feeling human being. His motives and methods may be in question, but he has also lost his marriage, with all of the once-held hopes and dreams. He also will have less time with his children, especially if they decide (and/or are encouraged) to take sides. He also will be shunned by people who want to take your side—your family and friends. He also will lose some social standing and respect of his peers. Many times that "other woman" thing doesn't work out and he finds himself isolated and lonely.

I was reading a book recently about wisdom in which the author was writing about his mother's divorce. He told his mother that a breakup was much harder on a man because men do not typically have the social networks that women do. I thought that was both interesting and sad. I believe that's another reason why men typically remarry so much sooner than women. They need someone to talk to. When my former husband first told me he wanted to leave, I asked him if he had talked with anyone (friend or family) about what he was doing. He said no, and I urged him to do so, but he never did. At the time I was thinking they might talk some sense into him, but still feel very strongly that he would have benefited from talking with someone who wasn't actually involved (his girlfriend). It is always good to have someone you care about (and who cares about you) to bounce ideas off of.

It is difficult when we are in pain to think about the pain of others, especially the ones we see as being the cause of our pain.

Rebecca Donovan

Remember that this man is one you loved with all your heart. Yes, this is painful, but he is still that person and the more you treat him with civility and fairness throughout this process, the better off you, he, and your children will be.

Bitterness – This is related to anger, only longer-term. Don't go there. It will make you sick and ugly and people won't want to spend quality time with you anymore. Even your best of friends will start backing away. Being around an angry bitter person is like inhaling noxious gas. Nobody wants to do that. How to recognize when you are bitter: When you are talking, do people stiffen, lean away from you, and seem uncomfortable? That could be bitterness coming from you. It could also be bad breath, which should not be ignored. Talk to yourself in the mirror about your breakup. Do you like the way your face looks? Do you say really mean, nasty things about your ex and/or his current partner? When talking about your situation, do you notice a little extra spray coming out of your mouth? Do you believe you were the innocent victim and want to make sure everyone everywhere knows it? Is that the same subject you want to talk about all the time? When you get done talking, do you notice your shoulders are all hunched up? Take a moment and think of someone you know who is bitter. Everyone knows some crotchety old person who is still mad about something that happened a lifetime ago. Do you want to be like that? I know I don't.

Zip It – If you're not sure if you should say something or not, the answer is almost always a resounding "not." If you start a sentence with "I really shouldn't tell you this," or "I was sworn to secrecy, but," or "I'm not sure if this is true, but," or "don't tell

Scorned, Torn And Reborn

anyone I said this," don't finish the sentence. Just ZIP IT! Words cannot be unsaid. Actions cannot be undone. They can, however, be regretted forever. When your mom said, "If you can't say something nice, then don't say anything at all," she knew what she was talking about. Integrity is that thing you do because you know in your heart it's the right thing. Look at yourself through the eyes of your children, or your grandmother, or some other person whose opinion you cherish. At the end of the day, it isn't about who's right or who won. It's about what you see when you look in the mirror.

Exercises

1. Make an effort to be kind to three people today. Write down their reactions.
2. Write a letter to yourself as if it is from your husband. How does he feel about the divorce?
3. Write out a conversation with a friend or family member where you tell them about the divorce. Try it without assigning any blame.

Visualization

Sit in a quiet place. Get comfortable. Take a deep breath in through your nose and blow it out very slowly through your mouth. With each breath you let out, imagine a part of your body completely relaxing. Start with your head. When you exhale, feel the tension leaving your head. Next, focus on your neck as you exhale. With each breath, move down your body until you get all the way to your toes. Continue to follow your breath as you imagine you are sitting on a couch in a room you know to be a safe and comfortable place. Sitting on the other end of the couch, facing you, is your husband. Focus on your breathing and remain calm. Find that place in your heart where kindness lives and speak to him from there. Tell him how you want your relationship with him to be from this point forward. Imagine his response, also coming from a place of kindness. Thank him and slowly walk away, feeling lighter with each step.

Chapter Eight
Family, Friends, and Other Support

> "Life is not a solo act. It's a huge collaboration, and we all need to assemble around us the people who care about us and support us in times of strife."
> — Tim Gunn

This is not the time to imagine you are Superwoman and can do this all on your own. Sure, you could, but why would you want to? We need the love, empathy, and support of our family, friends, and others—therapists, support groups, coaches, etc. You are going through a major upheaval in your life. Divorce is one of the most stressful experiences you will ever face. Let the people who care about you help you through it. It is not a sign of weakness to acknowledge that we need help. It is a sign of strength that we recognize how valuable that help will be.

My Story — Apart from a few close friends, I didn't tell anyone for a while that I was getting divorced. I was feeling embarrassed and humiliated. And I was in denial, hoping I would wake up and realize I had been having a bad dream, and everything would be okay. Obviously, everything was not okay, and I did start telling a few people. I started calling my friends. Then I kept calling them until, God bless them, they must have gotten so sick of me. But they stayed the course. They were there for me as I have been there for them.

My family was a slightly different story. I did not want my family to know why my husband was leaving me. Like I said, I was embarrassed. They thought very highly of my ex-husband, as he could be very charming and generally got the credit for any generosity we showed to family members, which was significant. I did not tell them any of the details of the divorce, so they might have assumed I was the one who messed up. I did not want my family to be discussing poor me, having pity for me, or saying negative things about my ex in front of my kids. The reason should not have mattered, but it did in my mind. It was two years before I told them what really happened. I told my nephew, and sure enough, just like a line of wobbly dominoes, the news was spread. They were genuinely shocked. If I had told them up front what the real deal was, I think they would have been more supportive. The truth is that I should not have felt embarrassed. I didn't have anything to be embarrassed about. He was the one who chose to take the coward's route, and I don't believe he was ever embarrassed about it.

A good friend recommended both a therapist and a support class. I took both recommendations. I saw the therapist for about a year but didn't really feel like it helped much. I quit going because I always felt worse after a session than I did before. That seemed a little backwards to me. I don't have anything against therapy or therapists in general; she just wasn't the best fit for me. The support class, however, a 12-week program, was very helpful. If I had known there was such a thing at that time, I would have skipped the therapist and hired a divorce coach. I knew people who had been through divorces (I, myself, had been through a divorce before), but not of the same nature as mine. A coach, or even a therapist or friend who really knew where I was coming from would have been a very welcome addition to my support circle.

Family – For most of us, our families will be very supportive of either our decision to divorce or what we are going through if it was not actually our decision. Many of us have a close family member who is also a confidante and trusted friend. This is a great time to reconnect with family from whom we may have, for one reason or another, drifted away. Some people may be afraid to tell their family anything. They fear judgment or feel shame about their "failure." This shame is not warranted. I know of one person who didn't tell his parents he was divorced and even went so far as to remove the "For Sale" sign from his yard when they came to visit in order to protect his secret. Your family may be your best source of comfort and understanding, and that's a bonus for you. While my family would surely have been more supportive if they had the whole story, I didn't want to get into it with them. The truth is that you do not owe anyone, family or otherwise, an explanation of why your marriage is not continuing. That is between you and your spouse, and your only obligation in the matter is to yourself and your children. If you don't wish to divulge the nitty gritty details, then in answer to the "What happened?" question, simply say, "It didn't work out" and leave it at that. If they continue to probe for details after you

Rebecca Donovan

have clearly told them you don't want to discuss it, then they are being rude and insensitive, and you are no longer obligated to be polite about it. That goes double for people outside of your inner circle. They may be curious, but it's just none of their business.

Friends – Unlike our family, we actually get to choose our friends. I found during this whole process (which can take a long time) that I have some amazing friends. There are several women in my life who I treasure with all my heart. They have been my salvation, and the only way to thank them is to offer the same loving support they gave me, no matter what they are going through. I have made other friends along the way who are very valuable to me as well, but that core of people who REALLY know you and love you anyway is priceless. They will listen to you as you repeat yourself, and cry, and rant and rave, and comfort you and encourage you when you feel despair and frustration. They will empathize and sympathize and tell you all the things you need (and sometimes just want) to hear. They are always there for you and don't keep score. If this does not describe any friends you have, then keep looking, because they are out there.

Sometimes we think people are our friends, only to be disappointed when we find out they are not. This mostly applies to those "couple friends." I did not get much attention from most of my married friends when I told them about the divorce. They probably didn't want to hear my sad tale and certainly didn't want to be in the position of taking sides. I was okay with that, but when my former husband and his girlfriend had a house-warming party within a few months of our divorce, I was a little hurt by the number of our couple friends who attended. Perhaps they were simply curious. Perhaps some people just really don't care who did what to who and why. They take the path of least resistance and gravitate toward other couples who invite them to parties. It's important to understand the distinction between friends and acquaintances. I thought I had a lot of friends when I was married. It turned out that I just had a lot of acquaintances. Acquaintances will rarely be people on whom you can depend.

In-laws — The reaction of my in-laws surprised me. It should have been obvious that they would not be in my support category, but for some inexplicable reason I thought they might be on my side. After all, I was the mother of their grandchildren. I had known them for eighteen years and considered them to be my family. It took years to forge a good relationship with my mother-in-law, and it was not an easy task. I don't know exactly how the tale was spun to them—I can guess I was the bad guy— but still I was taken aback to see them embrace the whole "out with the old, in with the new" concept. I saw them on a couple of occasions after the divorce, and while they were nice enough to me, they didn't seem to be bothered by the divorce or that I was no longer in their lives.

Once I was able to set aside my emotions and look at the facts, I found that this was not so surprising after all. He was their son, and they felt they needed to take sides and, of course, it would be his. He was always good to them, and they needed to support his decision. I get it. Looking at it from their eyes made me understand their reaction (or lack of it) better and not take it so personally. They say blood is thicker than water, and this is certainly illustrated in this type of situation. If you had a great relationship with your sister-in-law or brother-in-law, and are now confused by their distance, don't think it necessarily has anything to do with you. This is a confusing situation for everyone and, given some time, they may come back around. On the other hand, they may not. A sizable number of peripheral relationships are casualties of divorce. The more you and your partner can go through this process with dignity and grace, the less people will feel like they have to take sides. If you don't hate each other, other people will feel less compelled to hate on your behalf.

Empathy – This may be hard to get from people who have never experienced your particular brand of pain. The one person you will **not** get this from is your former partner, regardless of who left who, or how amiable your relationship may be at this point. I would keep going back to that place of insanity and try to get my ex-husband to empathize with me. I would start sentences with "How would you feel if..." and "Try to imagine..." Empathy was not his strong point to begin with, and even if it was, he didn't want to go there. He had made his decision and acted on it, and trying to associate with my pain would be of no personal gain to him, or any person in his position. We all have our own paths to take, and your husband is no longer on yours. In most cases, he doesn't really want to know what yours is, let alone help you take it. Cold as that may sound, it's the way it is. Find people who do know how you feel. You don't have to spend so much time explaining things to them. As you bump into people who are going through circumstances similar to yours, you have a chance to pay it forward with the empathy. It will help you to take your mind off of your own troubles every now and then to be present for someone else. There will come a time, however, when you don't need to spend so much time comparing notes. It has its healing purpose, but too much revisiting is not a good thing.

Vent — It's great to have friends who are understanding and have the time to listen to you vent. Sometimes you just need to blow off that steam. As with everything in life, however, moderation here is the key. Even the best of friends will grow weary of your tirades. Your dog will always listen to you no matter what. Cats, not so much. If you feel the need to rant and rave often, you might consider giving your pals a break and just take a drive. Back in the old days before Bluetooth, people would think you were a raving lunatic if you were talking (or raving) to yourself as you drive. Now everyone just assumes you are on the phone. It has been a most welcome technological breakthrough for those of us who like to self-converse. Another excellent way to vent is by writing. Take out your journal or a piece of notebook paper or a bar napkin and scratch out all the injustices you are suffering. Save your friends for when you really need them and don't wear them out with endless complaining.

Understanding — While it is so important to have people in our lives who are understanding, it is equally important to BE understanding. It's easy to think at this point that the ordeal we are experiencing is the worst thing that has ever happened to anyone. Meanwhile, there are other people who are suffering as well. When your child lashes out at you, try to imagine yourself in his or her position. They have had their world turned upside down, too. During the months between our separation and divorce, two of my good friends were also going through a divorce. It was a busy year for that. We need people to listen to us, empathize, sympathize, and tell us we are great and that everything will be okay. We also need to be mindful of those who need us. Sometimes we have to set aside our own pain to be present for someone else's, particularly our children, even if they're grown. Sharing the pain of others helps to put ours in perspective and know that we are not the only ones to feel this way.

Relationships – It is essential to maintain the relationships you have with other people. Some people will understand what you are going through, and more of them will not. Don't disregard a relationship simply because the person can't really relate to your situation. Value the relationship for what it's always been, even if you can't talk about your big breakup. Really, not everybody can or wants to hear it, and while it may be the biggest part of your life right now, you are MUCH MORE than that. Be *who you are* in your relationships, not just what you're going through.

Job – It's important to remember that your co-workers and your boss will be sympathetic and understanding of your situation right up to the point where it affects them. Then they won't. If you have to take some time off from work to collect yourself, and you can do so without jeopardizing your job, then do that. Don't talk about your former spouse or your divorce at work. Don't ask for special favors because you believe you are the first person to ever go through such a devastating upheaval in your life. Everyone has something that they are dealing with, and your situation, however much worse you believe it might be, doesn't make theirs go away. In this time of change, it is important to keep some things constant, and your job may be one of those things. Your place of employment is not the appropriate venue for venting.

Support Group – Around the time of my separation, a friend suggested I join a class for people who were coming out of relationships. It was based on a book entitled *When Your Relationship Ends* by Bruce Fisher. I wasn't always thinking clearly at that time, so it took some time to figure out why they called in the WYRE group. I thought it had something to do with being "wired in" or something. I felt kind of silly once I figured out it was an acronym, but I digress. This was a class/support group led by a local psychologist. It was one of dozens of classes he had led. That's a boatload of sad people. I found this group to be immensely helpful. Most of the people I knew while married were couples. Not only did I suddenly feel a little uncomfortable around couples, but I lived in a very conservative neighborhood where divorce was not something anyone wanted to "catch." This WYRE group provided a new group of friends who actually understood what I was going through. There were, at first, a lot of heart-rending shared stories and shared tears. Once we got to know each other and progressed through the class, we also shared a lot of laughter. There are a couple of people from that group I still consider friends. One of the benefits of a group like that is that no matter how tragic your story is, there is always someone with a bigger tragedy to bring yours into perspective. There was someone whose husband actually went on a website to FIND someone to cheat with, CHEATERS.com—I kid you not!— and carried on with that person for years. Another man's wife had a series of one-night stands without much discretion. One man's wife had left him for a woman. There were grandparents in the class who had been with their spouses for 30 years. The first few sessions were hard to get through because of the incredible pain that was so pervasive, but as the 12-week course moved on, the subjects became lighter. The weeks we had the themes on sex and dating were hilarious. These people didn't mind you talking about your experience or roll their eyes when you mentioned your ex. We all knew what it was like and how painful it was and how tremendously difficult it is to let go of a marriage, particularly one involving children.

It's true that misery loves company, but this group was much more than that. It was populated more by the "leavees" that the "leavers." In fact some of the "leavers" dropped out because it was uncomfortable for them. These types of things are not for everyone, but many people do gain a great deal from them.

Therapy – Like many people, on occasion I have turned to a therapist. Some people like it so much they continue to see their therapist for years. It can be very helpful. It may be just a very expensive sounding board. If it is not a good fit, it can actually be destructive. Personally, I was looking for a shorter term solution. Once you start into therapy, the problem is that you have to finish. If you quit before the issues are resolved, it can be worse than not going at all. If you open up this can of worms with your emotions and then quit while they are all out there raw and exposed, it can be very traumatic. I say this to let you know that therapy is not a quick fix. You have to be committed to see it through. That is why it is absolutely imperative to find the right therapist. Do your research. Get recommendations (not just the ones your insurance company recommends). INTERVIEW your top three. If you have to pick one because you hate the other two more, then keep looking. This is an investment that you are making in yourself and it should not be taken lightly.

Along the lines of therapy, I want to mention another book by Katherine Woodward Thomas, entitled *Conscious Uncoupling*.

This book goes a lot deeper into the subject of separating with dignity and coming out the other side a better person. The author has developed a process that has helped countless people through these circumstances and also has trained coaches around the country to do the same. Her program is designed so that you can do it on your own or with your husband. If you read it, I recommend that you do the exercises as well. You will always gain more from a book/program if you do the homework.

Coach – A coach is different from a therapist. The goal in coaching is generally to help you through a transition, like a divorce. Coaches are valuable assets for other life transitions as well, for example, the death of a partner or other loved one, children leaving home (or failing to), job loss, career changes, starting a new business, or re-entering the workforce after a long absence. The coaching process is driven by your goals and desires. You decide where you want to go, and the coach helps you with strategy and tactics to get you there. You work together to remove the blocks that hinder your progress. A certified coach has been through training and practice, but just like any other professional, not all are created equal. Do your homework and get recommendations. Have a phone conversation with a potential coach to make sure you are comfortable working with him or her. Depending on your needs and resources, this can be a short-term or a long-term relationship. I've been working with my life coach for about a year, and I wouldn't trade her for anything. She gets me. With a coach, it's all about you, which you can't always count on when your support comes from friends and family.

Your divorce is a big deal. Don't try to go through it all by yourself. Yes, you are a big girl, but big girls know when to ask for help. There are many people in your life who will help you. Let them. If you are a very private person and don't want your friends and family to be involved, then consider a support group, therapist, or coach. There are plenty of people in the world who have walked in your shoes and will be invaluable in helping you through this process.

Exercises

1. Write about a time when you helped someone through a difficult situation. You made their experience easier because you listened and understood. Think about and write down how it made you feel to help someone. When you let someone help you, it is a gift to them as well.

2. If you feel like you are wearing out your friends, consider a professional who can help you. Get a recommendation from a trusted source. Your lawyer or other divorce professional should be able to help you with this.

3. Write a letter to your favorite in-law. (If you don't have one, then that may be one of those bonuses of the divorce.) In the letter, tell them you value your relationship with them and hope to continue it. You can decide whether or not to send the letter.

Visualization

Sit in a quiet place. Get comfortable. Take a deep breath in through your nose and blow it out very slowly through your mouth. With each breath you let out, imagine a part of your body completely relaxing. Start with your head. When you exhale, feel the tension leaving your head. Next, focus on your neck as you exhale. With each breath, move down your body until you get all the way to your toes. Continue to follow your breath as you imagine you are standing in a field in a beautiful setting. Draw a circle around you and place the three people who are closest to you in that circle with you. Embrace them warmly and thank them for being there. Now draw a bigger circle and place three or four people in that circle that you consider to be good friends or close family. Greet each of them with a smile and thank them for being with you. Draw bigger and bigger circles to include all of the people you care about and who care about you. These are your support circles. Your young children and your husband will be in one of the outer circles. Older children may be closer in. Bask in the glow of love and support.

Chapter Nine

New Home

> "The ache for home lives in all of us, the safe place where we can go as we are and not be questioned."
> — Maya Angelou

Whether you stay in your current home or move to a new place, it is going to be a different home, with different dynamics. You need to make it your own. There are things you will want to hold on to and things you will want to discard. Give yourself some time to think about what you want. It's important to create a mix of what's comfortable with some new additions.

My Story — In our situation, my husband was the one to move out. I was not in a stable enough emotional state to handle changing my place of residence. I wanted the security of the familiar home where our family was established. I did not want my replacement to ever set foot in my house, let alone sleep in my bed. I have to assume that was not what she wanted, either, but I think my husband would have been fine with it. It was really weird for me the first time I ever had someone else in that bed with me, but I'm getting ahead of myself. The most important point for me was to have continuity for my sons. Brian moved to an apartment, taking only the things he needed and buying what we didn't have in duplicate. In Texas there is no legal separation status, so it's all still community property, which means I paid for half of his new stuff. In the grand scheme of things, it's hardly worth mentioning, but it did sting a little at the time.

As I said before, I helped with the move to the new apartment. I helped him set up his kitchen and the boys' room and showed him how to use the washer and dryer. Yes, seriously. He had a key to my house and gave me a key to his apartment. At that time it seemed like the whole family in two places thing wouldn't be so bad, and it wasn't at first. Brian was planning to get a house, but not until he could cohabitate with his girlfriend. His initial plan was to move in with her immediately. His lawyer advised him against that ill-conceived plan, so it was just him and the boys for a while. Once the divorce decree was in place, he just needed to wait until the paramour restriction ran its course.

Initially, my house didn't change much. Brian didn't even take all of his clothes. So he was there, but not there. We made an agreement in the decree that I could stay in the house for five years. It was paid off, so there was no mortgage, but he would pay for half of the property taxes and insurance, and any major necessary repairs. It seemed like a good idea at the time. Other than not wanting the girlfriend to be in my house, I didn't want my kids to have to move anything around. The upcoming divorce was enough for them to have to process without the added burden of moving. Even though our overnight time with them was evenly split, they would be at home with me after school every day, so I wanted that home to remain as stable as possible for them. I wanted to minimize the impact of the divorce as much as I could. There were definite advantages to this arrangement: 1) I didn't have to move right away; 2) I was at home, so the boys weren't alone after school; 3) I was the one in the place that my sons called home. There were also many disadvantages: 1) The house was too big and very expensive to maintain; 2) There was an inordinate amount of yard work; 3) I was living in a neighborhood where divorce was taboo; 4) I had a house full of memories and reminders; 5) Eventually, I would have to move a 4000 square foot house by myself (including all of Brian's crap that he had left behind) into a much smaller space.

I was still experiencing some denial about the house. I kept trying to figure out ways that I could keep it, but finally realized that was not the best thing for me, and not even for my kids anymore. After four years, we did sell the house and my little family of four (I count my dog) moved to an apartment for a short time before buying another house. In eleven years, we had accumulated a ridiculous amount of stuff in that house. I thought I was ahead of it, cleaning out closets and taking boxes and boxes to the trash and Goodwill, but it was overwhelming. The actual move was very emotional for both my boys and me. For me it was like getting divorced all over again. For them, as I grossly underestimated the amount of work and time it would take, it was just a lot of stress. When we subsequently moved from the apartment to the new house, I paid the movers to do it all, packing included, and it was so much easier and less stressful. It was definitely worth the extra cost.

If I had known then what I know now, would I have done things differently? I think I still would have stayed in the house, but for a shorter time. We divorced in 2008, which was a horrible time for the economy, and we most likely would have taken a beating on the sale at that time. I would have made more cosmetic changes sooner to define the space as mine, and I definitely would have started getting rid of extra stuff (especially his stuff) a lot earlier.

Standard of Living – Statistics on divorce always focus on the negative. There is less money. Everyone has to downsize. This happens out there every day, but that doesn't mean it has to happen to you as a permanent consequence, or that it even has to be negative. It doesn't mean you have to now live in poverty. When I talked about acceptance earlier, it doesn't mean you can't change anything. Some things you cannot change—that is true—but many more things you can. Accept that your relationship is over. Do not accept that you have no control over your destiny. Do not let the feelings of inadequacy that you will invariably experience during this time drive you to sell yourself short. It may take some time, but put a plan in place to improve your financial circumstances and follow it. This is where consulting with a financial planner can be helpful. I want to point out that not everyone who calls themselves a financial planner or advisor is actually going to help you. Most of them are trying to sell you something. They may try to sell life insurance and/or get you to put your money in some kind of fund. They get paid a commission when you place your money, so their income is not tied to the performance of the fund. A financial planner who specializes in divorce and charges you by the hour will help you with your financial decisions. This will include life insurance options (Who should be the owner of the policy? How much should it be for? etc.), which should be addressed in the divorce decree. They can help you set up a budget so that you will make a decision based on hard facts and dollars and cents rather than emotion. In the absence of a financial professional, any book written by Dave Ramsey can be very helpful with this aspect of the breakup.

There are professionals in other fields who specialize in divorce as well who can help you make informed decisions. Realtors and mortgage lenders are two examples. They can advise you on if and when to sell and help with issues involving establishing separate credit. Career counselors can help you if you have been out of the workforce for some length of time. With roughly 50 percent of marriages ending in divorce, there has been an entire industry created around it. While that may seem sad, it's good news for you to have so many resources available to you. I imagine how difficult it must have been for our mothers when they got divorced in the 1960s, when the divorce rate was around 25 percent. That's still a lot of divorces, but there was a huge stigma attached to them, so fewer options for help.

Home – Make your home your own. If your husband moved out and left a bunch of his crap, get rid of it. If he is in temporary quarters and can't take it all right now, make an agreement about how long you will store it for him. Do not do this indefinitely, as it impedes your ability to move forward. If the agreed upon time comes and goes, give him a deadline to come get it, and if he doesn't, then give it to your children if that's appropriate, or Goodwill, or a shelter, or sell it on eBay. Don't keep his belongings around as reminders of "what was." Brian took what he wanted and/or needed and left the rest for me to deal with. That was the easiest thing for him to do, and I did not stand up and make any demands about it, so that's on me. When we finally did move, all that extra stuff caused a lot of undo stress for me and my kids. Given all his remaining stuff, he probably should have helped with the move (I had helped with his), but again, I didn't ask and he didn't offer. I doubt the thought even entered his mind.

On the flip side, if you moved out of the residence you shared with your partner, take everything that belongs to you with you. There may be items that you can't divide until the divorce is actually final, but as soon as it is, get what's yours. Your ex may be angry and vindictive and may choose to dispose of something you treasure. Also—it's just bad manners to leave your castoff junk for your former spouse to deal with. Once you have your possessions, go ahead and make the new place your home. Even if it's much smaller and/or not as nice as what you're used to, don't live like a minimalist on a campout. If you're missing some pieces, buy what you need. If finances are an issue, go to garage sales. People sell furniture for all kinds of reasons, and if you take a little time, you can pick up some great items for a song. Buy some pictures or trinkets and new dishes. You don't want to come home every day to something that looks like a temporary shelter. I have a friend who moves fairly often for various reasons. She never unpacks more than bare essentials. Months after she's been living in a new apartment, there are still boxes everywhere. She doesn't know where anything is, and her place always looks like a refugee camp. This kind of chaos is bad for you. It adds unnecessary stress to your life. Put some time and effort into making your home a place of comfort and pride. Then invite people over.

Keepsakes – Throwing out unneeded and/or unwanted possessions can be very liberating, but don't be rash about cleaning out the attic, basement, garage, and closet. You may not be thinking clearly right now. When you are not thinking clearly, you should limit making these types of decisions until such time as you are in a more rational frame of mind. If you have to downsize right away, consider putting things in storage for a while and then look at them later. It is best not to go on a rampage and destroy everything the day your spouse moves out. Some things will retain some sentimental value and you need to have a clear head when deciding what to keep and what to heap. Give yourself some time to even out and then clean house. If it has been a year and you just can't manage to rid yourself of those romantic photos of the two of you in Cozumel or Florida, get some help. Have a trusted friend over for some packing and snacking. Hire a professional organizer to assist you. As time goes by, many of those keepsakes you thought held enormous sentimental value will lose their meaning. The purging process goes on indefinitely. Just this year I looked around my office and found that every family picture in there was from before the divorce. I quickly remedied that, putting up more current photos. As I write this I am preparing to move to another state, so I am continually amazed at some things I have moved three times already—that have never left the storage box. Yes, the purging process does continue.

Your physical surroundings are tied in with your emotional status. You think you are moving past the breakup and then you look over at the couch where the two of you used to snuggle and watch movies together, and the memory makes you cry. If you leave your house exactly as it was when he lived there with you, it makes it exponentially more difficult to move on with your life. Small changes can make a big difference. Change out the curtains or rearrange the furniture. Put away items that remind you of him and display what reflects YOUR personality. Get some input from your kids on new touches so that this home belongs to your new family subset.

Exercises

1. Look around the room you are in. Pick out three things you see that remind you of him and get rid of them, or at least put them away temporarily.
2. After you do the visualization below, go shopping for something for your home. It can be big, like a new couch, or small, like a new flower vase.
3. Replace old couple photos with current pictures of you or your kids, preferably doing something fun.

Visualization

Sit in a quiet place. Get comfortable. Take a deep breath in through your nose and blow it out very slowly through your mouth. With each breath you let out, imagine a part of your body completely relaxing. Start with your head. When you exhale, feel the tension leaving your head. Next, focus on your neck as you exhale. With each breath, move down your body until you get all the way to your toes. Continue to follow your breath as you imagine you are standing in an empty house. Slowly walk from room to room. If there are curtains or blinds, open them to let in the natural light. Now visualize how you want each room to look. Choose the flooring, the paint color, the furniture, and the artwork on the walls. Go slowly and don't leave out any details. This is your dream house, created exactly the way YOU want it to be. See the dishes, the sheets, and the towels. Find your favorite spot in the house and sit comfortably and quietly for as long as you want, feeling that is it completely yours.

Chapter Ten

Solitude and Loneliness

"Loneliness expresses the pain of being alone and solitude expresses the glory of being alone."
— Paul Tillich

When you have been living with other people for a long time, alone time can be a blessing or a curse, depending on how you feel in the moment. Yes, there will be times when you are lonely. In the early stages of your new solo adventure, you may find the loneliness to be overwhelming. There are many things you can do to combat or avoid that loneliness, but unless you are able to fill every waking moment with other people, loneliness will occur. There will also be times when you relish the solitude and use it to your great advantage. The less you focus on the past and the more attention you give to the present and future, the less you will be plagued by loneliness. You will learn how to use your time away from other people to jump start your growth into the person you want to be.

My Story — When I was married, it was unusual for me to have any time to myself at all. In fact, I used to plan trips by myself, just so I could be alone. When my husband moved out,

Rebecca Donovan

however, l was afraid of being alone. Not like, boogey man afraid, just afraid of being lonely. The last year or so that we were married, l remember feeling incredibly lonely, even while Brian was sleeping next to me. l didn't know at the time which type of loneliness was worse, alone lonely or with somebody lonely. l've since determined that the latter is much worse.

After Brian moved out, whenever my boys were spending time with him, l carefully scheduled get-togethers, and happy hours, and trips, and Thanksgiving, and Christmas so that l wouldn't have to feel lonely. Having activities and being around people was certainly good for me, but driving home at night after meeting with friends, l would dread walking into the empty house and feel somewhat panicked. l'm not sure at what point l stopped, but l probably felt like this for a couple of years. l spend much more time alone now than l did then, but l rarely feel lonely anymore. l love spending time with my sons, but l'm happy enough when they go, so that l have the place to myself again. Why did it take me so long to get over the lonely thing? Because in the very beginning l told myself l was going to be lonely. l talked myself into a panic over it. l thought if l didn't find a man right away or have lots of friends l was going to be too old and be alone forever. And that would just be the most awful thing imaginable. My subconscious took that seriously and ran with it, controlling my thoughts, feelings, and actions. l felt powerless to do anything about being lonely, so l tried to keep from being alone.

l'm so very happy that l got over that and learned to take control back from my subconscious again. lt was amazing the way l was self-sabotaging to stay stuck in the mindset l created for myself out of fear. The subconscious LOVES fear. These days l really don't mind being alone. Of course, l don't spend all my time alone. That would be unhealthy. I get out and see friends and do things with people. I spend time with my sons and my dog, but I am no longer afraid of being by myself. I only wish I could have figured it out sooner. There are so many things I wish I had figured out sooner.

Loneliness – This is unavoidable. There will be times when you feel incredibly lonely and sad, and you have to be present with those feelings. Being alone sometimes is a good thing. Too much of a good thing, however, can become a bad thing. It is hard to get back out there and make new friends and try new things. It is far easier to sit at home with a glass (or bottle) of wine and binge watch Netflix. Here's the hard fact: in order to have a social life, you have to actually leave your house. Oh, and also talk to people. Hmm... I have, over the years, been involved in several meetup groups (Meetup.com). There are groups for every interest under the sun. There are groups for Schnauzer owners, country and western dancing, knitting, moms with young kids, bowlers, hiking and camping, golfers, travel, and sisters of the summer moon— literally everything. It is a nice, generally safe way to make friends or at least be with people who share some of your interests. I have known people in these groups, however, who go all the time but never actually engage in conversation. Being alone in a crowd can be worse than being alone by yourself. It can feel like a big waste of time if you don't participate at some level. It may take a little trial and error before you find the right group or activity, but keep trying. There are a lot of different ways to meet new people. Take a class in something you've been wanting to learn or volunteer where you can make a difference. Don't wallow in your loneliness. Do something about it. Turn off the TV, get off your couch, leave your house, and go talk to people.

Melancholy — One time, years ago, I was reminiscing to a friend after a breakup from a boyfriend. I was telling her how I missed him and would like to see him again. I remember her sage words of wisdom. **"Are you frickin' insane?!"** He drank way too much, smoked pot constantly, and would disappear for weeks at a time. Breaking up with him was definitely in my best interest. Staying away from him was definitely in my best interest. She shook some sense into me, and I appreciated her for it. Sometimes we become melancholy, thinking about the "if onlys" and the "what might have beens." We go down that path of all the good memories, while conveniently fading out the bad ones. If you find yourself doing this, before you dial up your ex, go see that one reality-check friend that everyone must have. He or she will remind you of the facts surrounding the breakup. Once you have re-broadened your perspective, you can again make rational decisions.

Wishes — Wishes are nothing more than unfulfilled disappointment. They don't get us anywhere, most especially if we are wishing about things that have already happened. We cannot wish away that which has already come to pass. We also can't wish our way to a better life. "I wish I could lose 10 pounds." "I wish my ex would dump the person who broke us up." "I wish I had a better job." "I wish I wasn't getting a divorce." "I wish I could go to sleep and wake up when it's over." Goals, clearly stated, written down, reviewed, and acted upon, can, however, get us where we want to go. To quote Robert Frost: "The only way out is through."

Yearning — This is a little bit like wishing. Yearning is wanting or longing for something that is just out of reach. You think you

124

want it, but don't truly believe you can have it. If you find you are yearning for something, explore it and ask yourself why you don't think you can have it. If it's REALLY not attainable, like deciding at age 50 to be a professional basketball star or an astronaut, then let it go. Then think about why you are yearning for that thing, and what you might do instead that fills that need. Maybe you can write science fiction books about space travel. Maybe you can join an over-50 basketball league or coach kids. If it IS attainable, then turn your yearn into a goal and work a plan to make it happen.

Solitude – When I talked about loneliness, I gave some suggestions on things to do to avoid being alone. Solitude is different. It is the good side of being alone. It gives you time to reflect, read, write in your journal, take long walks, clean your house (ugh!), etc. I believe every person should live alone at some point in their life. You must be able to be completely comfortable with your own company before you can be fully present in someone else's. The more you like yourself, the more you have to offer to another and the more able you are to receive what they offer. I mentioned before that I've been working with a coach for a while now. Many of the things I work on with her require some alone time. The first thing I do every morning when I get up is go for a walk. If my dog is home (she still spends time with my ex), then I walk with her. Otherwise I go by myself. This is an excellent time to be present and enjoy solitude. I also write in a journal—three pages every morning, plus a page for gratitude. I enjoy sitting on my back porch drinking coffee. Admittedly, I do spend a little time with a glass of wine and some Netflix. I have found a good balance between being with other people and being alone. There is great value in both.

Courage – It's going to take some courage on your part to get through this period in your life in a dignified manner. It's easier to give over to the negative emotions you have and questionable advice you will receive, easier to stay angry and assign blame. Everything else discussed in this book takes courage to effectively pursue. At times it will seem like the courage of a superhero, but at the end of the day, it's unlikely you will be hailed as such. I definitely did not do everything I suggest in this book, and many of the good things I did took longer than they should have. Still, I look back and feel good about most of it. While some of my good friends recognize and applaud my efforts, mostly I don't think I got credit for much of it, especially from my ex-husband, but that's okay. The thing about dignity and integrity is that YOU know. I know what I did. I know the sacrifices I made and the restraint I managed to employ. For whatever is left over, we can forgive ourselves, learn from it, and move on.

Exercises

1. Make a list of five things you like doing by yourself.
2. Think of a time when you were married that you wished you had some time to yourself. What would you have done with the time?
3. Plan something for yourself that you have always enjoyed doing by yourself (walking, shopping, crafts, etc.).

Visualization

Sit in a quiet place. Get comfortable. Take a deep breath in through your nose and blow it out very slowly through your mouth. With each breath you let out, imagine a part of your body completely relaxing. Start with your head. When you exhale, feel the tension leaving your head. Next, focus on your neck as you exhale. With each breath, move down your body until you get all the way to your toes. Continue to follow your breath as you imagine you are sitting alone in a room. The room is warm and filled with natural light, and there is a doorway on the other side of the room. You feel calm and comfortable. A beautiful, poised, impeccably dressed woman walks in the room and greets you warmly. You know her. She is a part of you. Next, a little girl comes bouncing in, full of playful energy. She smiles and waves hello. You know her as well. She is a part of you, too. One by one, people come in the room who represent different parts of you. Some of them are strong. Some of them are weak. Some are pleasant. Some, not so much. But you love each and every one of them, because they are you. As you embrace them, the light fills the room until you all become one, and you know that you are never alone.

Chapter Eleven

A New Social Order

"There is nothing noble in being superior to your fellow man; true nobility is being superior to your former self."
— Ernest Hemingway

It's time to embrace the different turns your life will be taking now. Many changes have already occurred, and many more are to come. The status quo is out. A new social order is in. Unless you had a separate and loyal friendship with one half of a "couple friend," chances are high that this couple will no longer be in your social group. I have found that many married women always have some level of distrust of their husbands tucked away. They do not want available women hanging about. Insecurity, you ask? Why, yes, but it is often not without merit. In my observation, there are a great many married men who could be persuaded to cheat with a small amount of encouragement. My ex-husband was a perfect example. I was pretty sure that he would never cheat on me, but he convinced himself that was the way to go. It's a combination of ego, a lack of fulfillment, and the ever-enticing greener grass. There are a substantial number of studies done and books written on why men cheat, and it's far too complex a subject to go into here. Suffice it to say, many married women have a wary eye and do not want a bunch of single women around. That's not to say you can't still have friendships with married women. Just understand that your worlds no longer line up the way they used to. It's time to move forward and find your new tribe.

My Story – My separation and subsequent divorce went along pretty quickly, as I've said. There was a wine club that my husband and I had belonged to for several years in our neighborhood. Once a month, four to six couples would get together and try new wines. We rotated houses, and the hosts would choose the wines for the evening. It was always a lot of fun and something we looked forward to each month. In addition to wine club, we also socialized on occasion with one or more of the couples. After a few years, you get to know people pretty well. At least you think you do. The last wine club we had was at our house. I already knew Brian was leaving me, but we hadn't told the kids, so very few other people, including our wine club, knew. After we told our kids and before the next wine club meeting, I sent an email to the group, explaining that Brian and I were getting divorced and would no longer be participating in wine club. Two out of five of the women responded with a short note. Only one woman ever reached out to me after that. She and I remained friends for a few years after that, but as I said, our worlds didn't line up anymore.

At the time of my divorce, although two of my friends were also getting divorced around the same time (these are both still very good friends), I did not have any single friends. As I found I also didn't have much going in the way of married friends (locally), it was time to go friend hunting. I found what I needed in the support group I mentioned earlier in the book. During the summer of the classes and into the next couple of years, this group of people became my tribe. Over time we have all gone our separate ways. As we all healed and moved on (several have remarried), we had less and less in common. Some I keep up with only on Facebook, but we all have a special place in our hearts for each other because we came together in a time of immense mutual need. We kept each other up, listened to each other, and showed up for each other. There was a great deal of sorrow and heartache, and in some cases we literally saved each other.

Over time I have made other friends, both married and single, male and female, through various social Meetup groups and business networking groups. I find it interesting at my age that many people, although they go to the various Meetups, don't seem to have the time or energy to form and nurture actual friendships. I've never been so popular that I didn't think I could use another friend, and I'm always open to that possibility. To think otherwise is to limit your own growth potential. Valuable friends can come from the most unexpected places, and will enrich your life in amazing ways.

Drinking – I am an avid wine drinker. I love good wine and drink it more days than not. When I first got separated, I was drinking much more than I was used to, however. I was going out a lot more, which generally involved drinking, and would drink more at home as well. This is okay in the short term as long as you are not driving impaired and it doesn't interfere with your job or affect your children if you have them. When I say short term, however, I do mean SHORT term. Alcohol may dull your senses in the moment or make you think you are more charming or humorous, but it is not a substitute for anything you feel you

are now missing. Too much of it will affect you in very negative ways. For example, say you are thinking about your ex. Maybe you are really missing him and feeling melancholy, or perhaps you are an angry drunk and are feeling the pain. So you decide to call. Drinking and dialing is NEVER a good idea. We all make the most moronic statements when drinking, and more often than not, regret them later. Drink if you must, but **do not dial that phone**. The same goes for texting. Think twice, thrice even, before hitting that SEND button. Every phone should have one, but I have yet to see an UNSEND or OH CRAP! WHAT WAS I THINKING? button. Moderation is absolutely my mantra, and it certainly applies here. If you find that you are drinking a lot more than you used to, slow down or stop completely. Take a hard honest look at what you are doing and what the benefits are versus the detriments. The same goes for any other substances you may be using, be it sleeping pills, or pot, or whatever. None of that is a long-term substitute for your "old life." Abuse of these will only inhibit your ability to move forward.

Read — Read some books. I know that's what you are doing right now, so congratulations on that. There are a lot of books out there about relationships and divorce and dating and parenting. A number of them are even good. Almost all of them have something you can take away to improve your attitude, mental health, etc. When you do find yourself alone at home or the coffee shop or on a lunch break, grab a book instead of the pint of rocky road in the freezer. It will be more helpful than reruns of Frasier or Friends (although those are pretty good, too). If you get tired of the self-help books, branch out. Read novels, biographies, bird watching books—anything to expand your mind and get you out of the pity party.

Develop − Expand your intellect, your social skills, your friendships, your professional networks. For your intellect, take a class at the local college, or if you feel especially ambitious, finish that degree or start a new one. Not ready for such a large step? Do the crossword puzzle or Sudoku or some other brain enhancer. You may be the life of the party and require no brush-up on your social skills. For many of us who have relied on "couple friends," which often turn out to be more acquaintances than friends, we are not particularly comfortable going out and making new friends. If you are young, you probably still have many single friends to socialize with. Certainly, if you have some married friends who you still want to spend time with (my personal experience with married friends does not dictate yours, of course), you shouldn't forego your friendships with them. It is very helpful (and hopeful) to spend time with people who have a good, solid relationship, but too much of that will make you feel like the third or fifth wheel. Gravitating toward your old couple friends can also be a form of denial. I had one friend who had grown up in the local area and knew a lot of people. Every time we went out we would run into some couple she and her husband had been friends with. They had been part of a country club crowd, and she missed the status of that, so whenever she came upon someone from her old world, she would blow me off to insert herself into their space. Yes, that did get annoying and we stopped hanging out. I think she rejoined the country club, but I will tell you, it probably won't be the same. I kept our club membership for a while to play golf, but didn't find it very welcoming. Again, that is an individual thing, and if you play golf or tennis, that might be a great place for you to socialize. But you will still need some single friends. Do something new on a regular basis to get to know people. Take a class in something you want to learn, and kill two birds with one stone. Join an exercise class or gym. Do volunteer work. Join a professional organization and get involved. This covers new friends AND professional networks.

Fun – You have been (and are still) going through a lot. Go do something fun. Take a trip with a friend. If you don't have friends to travel with, join a travel group. I belong to one called Adventures for Solo Travelers. This is not some kind of hook up group. It is a group of solo travelers, who go on trips together. The age range of that group is generally 40s and 50s. They will pair you with a roommate, or you can pay a premium to have a private room. Personally, I like the roommate arrangement. I have made some good friends that way. A little research will reward you with groups that share your interests. Go to wine country. Go skiing. Many cities have ski clubs that go on trips. Go river rafting or fishing or camping. Go to the carnival or local fair. Dress up for Halloween and crash a party. Throw a party. Decorate for holidays. Go shopping for something completely frivolous. Go to the animal shelter and play with the puppies and kittens. Go see a kids movie (they can be pretty good) or a comedian. Play softball, or kickball, or volleyball, or basketball. Join a bowling league. Take a Tango class. Go to a ceramics workshop and make a bowl. That's a boatload of suggestions. Surely you can find something that tickles your fancy. Do something for no other reason than just to have fun. It will feel great.

Holidays – No matter how many months you have between the big separation and "THE HOLIDAYS," it will undoubtedly cause you some angst. It is a happy, cheerful, joyous time of year and also unbelievably stressful for most people under the best of circumstances. When you add the burden of a breakup to your holiday "to do" list, it can be quite debilitating. This is the time when it is essential that you stay connected. Connect with yourself using meditation, yoga, acupuncture, tai chi, massage, or just plain old exercise. Eat healthy food and take your vitamins. Drink nice herbal teas and take a hot bath. Connect with friends and family. Spend time with other people. If you find yourself alone for the holidays, volunteer at a homeless shelter or orphanage or at the very least foster some homeless dogs or cats for a few days. Try to get in the festive spirit by decorating your home. If you don't have children and don't want to go all out, at least put a wreath on your front door and buy yourself some peppermint chocolate candy. Get into the spirit of holiday giving with any number of community programs to help people who are less fortunate than you. Yes, there are people less fortunate than you. Be out among people, but don't sit at the end of the bar smoking cigarettes and crying in your beer. While it may seem so, this is definitely not a time to be drinking and dialing. The last thing you need at this point is pity. I'm not sure, but I don't think pity and respect can coexist.

I made sure in the divorce decree that I would have my kids with me on that first Christmas morning. That holiday season was hard for me. Christmas was always such a big deal at our house. I will admit to sending a couple of "poor, poor, pitiful me" emails to my ex-husband. He was actually somewhat sympathetic. He wasn't a complete psychopath, after all.

There are some good points to ponder about the first holidays as a new single person. You do not have to put up with annoying in-laws. You have a lot less shopping to do, unless your spouse did all that for your side of the family and now you have to do it. If you were the spouse doing that, then you have a lot more free time since you don't have to find the perfect gift for his Aunt

Martha, who never appreciated it anyway and always called you "my dear nephew's wife" because she couldn't remember your name. That's still better than my first husband's aunt, who always called me by his previous girlfriend's name. Come to think of it, his mother actually did that, too. Hmmm.

Unfamiliar — There are going to be times when everything may seem unfamiliar and uncomfortable. Your life has been turned upside down, and navigating this new path will at times feel very strange.

You may be moving to a new neighborhood. Ask your new neighbors for suggestions on dry cleaners, Chinese food and pizza delivery, best grocery stores, etc. Two things are accomplished here. One, you have a reason to talk to your neighbors, who just might turn into friends, and two, you don't have to go hunting for all those things, which will reduce your overall stress.

Having to go out on your own and mix it up with strangers to make new friends may be something you haven't done in a long time. If you are fortunate, you have a place you go regularly (like your job), where it's easy to get to know people you see every day. If you don't have that, it is more of a challenge.

It's always a good thing to push your comfort zone just a little. Sometimes we have to push a little harder. If this is difficult for you, start small. Try going into the bank or fast food restaurant instead of the drive-through. Give a little more time to random interactions you have with people in everyday situations, and you will find that they get easier. Take the time to make eye contact with the sales person or cashier. Ask them how they are doing, and then actually listen to the answer.

On the other hand, if you are really good at this, then no problem. Wherever you are on the party spectrum, relax and enjoy yourself. Strike up conversations with people who are completely different from what you are used to. People are just people, and the more you talk to them, the more you find you have in common.

Smile — Hey, turn that frown upside down. ☺ Seriously, if you make the muscles of your face turn your mouth up on the corners, it actually releases endorphins that make you feel better and reduce stress. I'm not making this up. It's supported by science. Don't take my word for it, though—give it a try!

Spirituality — Whether or not you are a religious person, the thought that we are part of something larger than ourselves is comforting. You don't have to believe in God, per se, in order to be spiritual. It can just be the belief that we are all somehow connected. I consider meditation to be a spiritual practice, as well as yoga. Anything that enables us to look inside ourselves in a positive way can be very healing. I have studied many different religions and find that almost all of them have the same central theme. That is to love yourself and be nice to other people. Everything else pretty much falls into place. When I read spiritual books, I feel connected. For example, when I read books written by Buddhist monks I feel a sense of well-being. You do not have to subscribe to the particular philosophy of the author. The beauty of a good spiritual book, regardless of its origin, is that it speaks to the reader on a personal level. You can pick up the Bible, Kabbalah, or any book on consciousness, meditation, yoga, reincarnation, etc., and get something positive from it.

The move from being one half of a couple to being one whole of yourself is challenging. It's important to get out and do things with current and new friends. While many of your married friends will fade away, you will find which ones were real friends. Take this time to get out there and meet new people. Do some fun things that you've always wanted to do. Explore and expand your horizons by reading, taking classes, and talking to different types of people. Your social life will definitely change, but only you can decide to make it for the better.

Exercises

1. Make a list of five things you are interested in. Go online and find at least one group you can join in one of those interests.
2. Actually go to a meeting or event for the above.
3. Call a friend you've lost touch with and make a date for coffee or lunch.

Visualization

Sit in a quiet place. Get comfortable. Take a deep breath in through your nose and blow it out very slowly through your mouth. With each breath you let out, imagine a part of your body completely relaxing. Start with your head. When you exhale, feel the tension leaving your head. Next, focus on your neck as you exhale. With each breath, move down your body until you get all the way to your toes. Continue to follow your breath as you imagine you are standing alone at a party. There is a crowd of people with friendly faces, all having a good time. You know a few of them, but mostly they are strangers. You feel calm and welcome and self-assured. Look around until you see someone you know who is talking with someone you don't know. Walk up to the person you know and greet them with a smile. Exchange pleasantries and then turn to the person they are talking to, smile, and introduce yourself. Smiling back at you, they introduce themselves. Say their name to help you remember. Ask them how they know the person you know or the party host. As the conversation with those two draws to a natural conclusion, excuse yourself and find someone else you know. Do the same thing there. Now look around and find someone you don't know who is laughing. Walk up to that person with a smile and introduce yourself. Engage in short conversation and then repeat this process until you have met most or all of the people in the room. Each time you do this it becomes more and more comfortable. Choose your favorites and go back to talk to them again. Every person you greet with a smile gives you one in return. You feel warm and included.

SECTION III

After the Divorce

REBORN

Chapter Twelve
Finding Closure and What You Really Want

"If the door closes, quit banging on it! Whatever was behind it, wasn't meant for you. Consider the fact that maybe the door was closed because you were worth so much more than what was on the other side."
— Anonymous

At some point you will think you have done a great job of letting go. The divorce is final. You've started going out. You've made some new friends. Things are looking up. You think you have let go, but there may be some little issue that is keeping you from doing that. You may find out there is something big that you have not completely let go. Whatever this thing is, it's keeping you stuck and not letting you move forward. It may be hard to put your finger on it, but things just seem unfinished. You may have a nagging sensation that you have forgotten something. Reflect on your thoughts and actions. How much are you still talking about him? Do you have to make a concerted effort not to? Do you wake up in the middle of the night thinking about him (in a good, bad, or even neutral way)? You need to find closure.

My Story – Letting go was something I thought I had done quite nicely—accepted the facts and moved on. Then it hit me that I had not, in fact, moved on. I was still hanging on to the idea that there was some special bond with my former husband. About a year after our divorce, I found myself writing an email to Brian in which I asked that he stop some particular thing that he was doing. I don't even remember what it was. His response was to write back a very hateful email, designed to hurt me. It did hurt me because I was still giving him that power. In addition, I knew him well enough to know that if I told him he was doing something wrong, he would react with anger. It was how he always reacted to that. As I read the email again, I realized that I had not ever really let go. I still wanted some acknowledgement or approval from him. I had accepted the fact that we would not ever be together and had long since passed the point where I actually even wanted that. But still, there I was, looking for something from him that I *never* did get and *never* would get. I thought we could remain friendly, but in order to get closure I realized I needed to distance myself from him. Once I realized that I had not fully let go, it was much easier to actually do so. It was not something that happened overnight, however. It was drawn out for me for a lot of reasons, mostly because the divorce didn't give me the clear separation that it should have (like if I had listened to my attorney). I don't think I felt like there was real closure until I sold and moved out of the house we had shared, almost four years after the divorce was finalized.

Since that time I have been on a journey of self-discovery. My life has taken many twists and turns, and I have done things I would not have thought I could do before. The main thing I have been doing all these years is figuring out what I really want. I am on the right track, without a doubt, but this, too, is an ongoing process, as it should be.

Getting Closure – It is essential with any ending, whether it is a divorce, or the death of a loved one, or the end of a job or friendship, to have closure. You need to be able to finish one chapter so you can turn the page and begin another. Some couples have been known to actually have a ceremony to finalize this chapter. This can be just the two of you, or it can include friends and family. If you are both ready to move forward and can be on friendly terms, this is a powerful way to say goodbye to the couple and hello to the individuals. It also serves the purpose of letting people know that you are in a good place and that it's okay to be friends with both of you. During this ceremony, you talk about the things you shared and the happy times you had. Reflect on the gifts you have given each other and the warmth that you will always feel for this person. The people in your life will appreciate the relief that comes with not having to choose between you. Other people will be confused because they don't understand this kind of divorce and think there should be animosity and unrest. Maybe don't spend much time with those people. They will only hinder your personal progress.

It may not be possible to have a ceremony of this sort for a number of reasons. If that's your situation, then do something substantial for yourself to clearly mark this passage. If only in your mind, say goodbye to him with a positive attitude. Thank him for his contribution to your life and for loving you and caring about you. If the relationship was abusive and there just isn't anything nice to say, simply thank him for not being in your life anymore. You can write him a letter and ceremoniously burn it. The purpose of this exercise is to close the chapter. Do what makes sense for you, but if it is not possible for you to do it without anger and resentment, perhaps you can engage the help of a friend, therapist, or coach.

Forgiveness – The ability to forgive will free you in uncountable ways. First and foremost, if you are holding on to guilt or blaming yourself, you must forgive yourself. If you are a religious person, that may include prayer and talking with your minister. A therapist or life coach can also provide guidance and support as you explore self-forgiveness. There's no shortfall of books written on the subject of forgiveness. Amazon lists over 16,000 of them. Look deep inside your soul and offer up forgiveness. No amount of guilt or remorse will change what has happened in the past. You can only learn from the experience and do better today and tomorrow.

After any necessary self-forgiveness, you can begin to forgive your former husband. He might actually ask you for it. You may not think he deserves it. Maybe he doesn't, but it isn't really for him, it's for you. You can make a ceremony out of forgiving yourself and your former husband if you wish, or incorporate it into your closure ceremony if you're doing one. There may be other people involved that you'd like to forgive as well. Sometimes friends, in-laws or family members will put themselves in the middle of your business out of some misguided good intentions (or not). If there was another woman (or man) involved in the divorce process, you might consider forgiveness of that person. You will probably come to realize that this person has done you a favor.

While forgiveness is a necessary step in order to move forward with your own life, it should not be done with haste. You must acknowledge the full impact of this "uncoupling" process with all of its periphery before you can realize the benefit of forgiving this person. I jumped in to forgive my husband way before he was done with the things I needed to forgive. Once you have all the information in line, then you can better appreciate the gift of forgiveness. For this truly is a gift that you are giving to yourself AND to the recipient of your forgiveness.

Jealousy – That little green monster rears its ugly head sometimes when you least expect it. You're doing good just to make it to the office every day, and on the one day you finally agree to go with your friends to happy hour, there sits your former husband with a DATE! *Do not* A) run to the bathroom to hide and cry, B) loudly introduce yourself as the one that got away, or C) sulk in the corner while shooting ice darts at your ex and the date. *Do* inconspicuously steer your friends toward the other side of the room where you are out of direct line of sight and have a good time with them, while *not* casting furtive glances in the ex's direction. You will find yourself feeling jealous or envious over things you never thought of, like your neighbors' "perfect marriage" or that skank that married your high school sweetheart, or the fact that you are way cooler/better looking than your sister/cousin/friend/neighbor's Aunt Mary, so why are they happy and you're not? Remember, just because the grass looks greener on the other side of the fence does not necessarily mean it is. Sometimes when you look closer you realize what's causing it to look green is just fresh cow patties.

It is inevitable that your former husband is going to date. It's also quite possible that he will remarry, with what may seem like remarkable haste. The truth is that as much as men complain about marriage or pretend to want to avoid it, they do not, as a general rule, like to be alone. When either of these things happen, regardless of where you are in your personal recovery journey, it's going to smack a little. Maybe a lot. There isn't anything to do about it. He is free to do what he wants. The question for you to answer then is, what do YOU want?

Query – Ask questions—lots of questions. What do I want? What do I need? Where do I want to go? What is my passion? If you find yourself answering those questions with "my husband," ask them again until you get a better answer. Also ask yourself what you don't want. What do you never want to do again? Where do you draw the line in the sand? What are you not ever going to put up with again? Ask yourself where your boundaries are and commit to honoring them.

Xenogenesis – I include this not only because I like cool words that start with the letter "x," but also because it is an important factor in the quest to find what we want. Xenogenesis is the production of an individual completely different from either of its parents. This is something many of us strive for, but rarely achieve. If you've ever had someone, like your husband, make the mistake of accusing you of being "just like your mother," you know what I mean. The harder we try to be unlike our parents, the more we seem to mirror them. We have all heard words come out of our mouths that sound identical to the ones that made us cringe as children. Many times problems will come up in our romantic relationships when we try to get from our partners that which we needed but could not get from our parents. In your self-reflection, it is necessary to understand these unmet needs to help prevent you from becoming your parents. Unless you had the most amazingly perfect set of parents. In that case, carry on.

Want — This is the time to figure out what it is that you really want. There are plenty of books available that are written on this subject, as well. I recommend a book by Danielle LaPorte, entitled *The Desire Map*. In this book, the author takes the reader through a series of exercises to help them determine what they really want. The premise is not just what you want to accomplish. The question is, how do you want to feel? It's one thing to say, "I want to move back to my home town in the mountains." It is another to say, "When I am in the mountains I feel connected to the Earth and all its beings. I want to feel that sense of connection and vitality that I get in the mountains." This way of looking at what we want separates what we think we should want, or what other people think we should want, from what we ourselves really want. Many people go through their entire lives without ever discovering what it is that they truly want. This is one reason why so many relationships are unsuccessful. How can you possibly get what you want out of a relationship, a job, travel, anything, if you don't know what that is? This is your opportunity to figure it out. It's not about being selfish. It's about finding out who you are and what it will take for you to be happy. Everyone around you benefits from that, especially your children.

This is also the part where you get the freedom to DO what you want. Not everything about divorce has to be bad. The freedom can be exhilarating. This is your time to explore and do the things you couldn't do before. I used to ski when I was younger, and for one reason or another, my husband would never go with me. As soon as I got divorced, I joined the local ski club and still take trips with them almost every year. I love it! It's part of who I am. Maybe you like camping and your ex-husband had a phobia about ticks. Maybe you've always wanted to try mountain biking, skydiving, or scuba diving and were discouraged by your spouse for whatever reason. Make that trip to Machu Picchu, or Vietnam, or Branson, MO if that's your thing. Take this time to be who YOU are and do what YOU want. We'll explore this in more detail later.

Excuses – For every suggestion in this book or the ones you get from friends and family or things you just know you should be doing, there are multiple excuses that will get in your way. "I don't feel good," "I'm tired," "I don't have time," "I can't afford it," "I'm embarrassed," "I'm not good at that," "I'm afraid of ...," "I'll do it when..." Stop making excuses for why you can't get on with your life. This is about you moving forward with dignity. It is up to you to make that happen. People will help you and encourage you, but no one is going to do it for you. Eliminate the words "I can't" from your vocabulary and never utter them again.

It's crucial to have closure to one chapter of your life before you open up another one. Make a point of doing this with some sort of ceremony, whether that is with other people or simply by yourself. Offer forgiveness to those who have wronged you. Don't forget to forgive yourself first. Then you can set about figuring out what you want. And then go get it.

Exercises

1. Think of something you have not let go of yet. Write down what you need to do to let that thing go.
2. Perform a ceremony by yourself or with others to get closure and offer forgiveness.
3. Make a list of three things you want to do. Write beside them how it will make you feel to do them.

Visualization

Sit in a quiet place. Get comfortable. Take a deep breath in through your nose and blow it out very slowly through your mouth. With each breath you let out, imagine a part of your body completely relaxing. Start with your head. When you exhale, feel the tension leaving your head. Next, focus on your neck as you exhale. With each breath, move down your body until you get all the way to your toes. Continue to follow your breath as you imagine there is a place you've always wanted to go. See yourself going to the airport and getting on a plane. You smile in anticipation as you take your seat. Where is the plane headed? Imagine what you will do when you get there. Imagine the weather there and the clothes you're wearing. How does it make you feel? Sink into that feeling and imagine feeling that way all the time.

Chapter Thirteen

Co-Parenting

> "A child cannot have too many people who love
> them and want to help them succeed."
> — Anonymous

The ease of co-parenting will have its ebbs and flows, depending on the players involved and the circumstances du jour. It's important to establish an agreement with your ex-husband during the divorce and put that into the decree. You can always change the way you do things if you both agree, but it will save you a lot of headaches and arguments to have your fallback in writing. When other people enter the arena—and they will—they'll come with their own ideas about parenting. You or your ex-husband may be influenced by these well-meaning (I hope) individuals, but it's important for BOTH of you to remember who the actual parents are. If you have handled your divorce with grace and integrity, it will be easier to maintain the flow with co-parenting your children. Once there is a romantic partner on either side who is involved in the parenting decisions, it would be a good idea for everyone to meet and make friends. This may be difficult for you, especially if this person is "the other woman," but it is in the best interest of the kids for you to get along.

Remember, as irritating and inconvenient as the two-household situation is for you, it's nothing compared to what your kids have to put up with. Regardless of whose idea this whole thing was, or what the kids know about that, you will sometimes get the brunt of their frustration. Homework and favorite sweaters left at the other house, your schedule interfering with their social life, their forgetting what day they are where, and so on, will all be your fault sometimes. Try to be patient and understanding and refrain from flinging back at them that it's really all their dad's fault—even if you believe it is. The more you are in amicable communication and the closer the two houses are to each other, the easier these mini disasters will be to contain.

My Story – It's difficult to tell my story of the saga of co-parenting without sounding a bit like a whiney martyr. But I'll try to leave those parts out. I mentioned before that the relationship with Brian's wife started out reasonably well given the circumstances. I thought we could be one of those modern families that could let bygones be bygones and embrace the new reality. Initially, Brian agreed with me and seemed relieved that I might be willing to do that; he was especially happy when I first met with her. I still believe that vision would have been possible, but the well was poisoned along the way. I'm not sure exactly what happened, but I have a sneaky suspicion that Brian was at the forefront, creating divisiveness where it didn't need to be. He had a habit when we were married of always making a point to let me know that he found other women attractive, whether it was a stranger in a restaurant or our friends and neighbors. Obviously we all are human and we find people other than our spouses attractive. It was more than that; he wanted me to know he had options. A mutual friend confirmed that he also did this to his new wife. The problem, I think, was he used me as the alternative—to make her think I was still an option. I was not, but she didn't know that. I believe that may have been the start of the rift.

I also believe Brian expected his new wife to be an exact replacement of me, including all of the parenting. If he stayed true to form, he probably made comparisons, widening the rift. She became paranoid about any contact Brian and I had. He quit participating in some of our sons' activities because I was also involved and she didn't want us in the same place at the same time. He was on a strict time clock when he came to pick up or drop off the boys. She insisted that she be copied on ALL correspondence between him and me. I complied with that a few times, but stopped because I got tired of her nasty replies to me.

I never once said any harsh words to her, and I bent over backwards to accommodate them. I was always willing to be flexible in the hope that it would help build the relationship. The one time I asked her for help, however, she refused. Even now, after all this time, if I run into her, I say hello and she ducks her head and goes the other way.

All of this would have been tolerable if she had at least been good to my kids. She wasn't. When I would drop them off at their house, she wouldn't even greet them, much less attempt to have a relationship with them. She makes it very clear at present that she doesn't like my older son. She makes it clear to *him*. She has two children of her own, whom my sons barely know. Unlike many new step-parenting situations, she had two boys coming in who were completely open to establishing a relationship with her. She had the perfect opportunity to embrace them and build a lifelong bond that would have enriched her life. It's sad for her that she chose not to because they are two pretty awesome people.

The good news is that we all survived. The boys are grown, and I no longer have to have any interaction with her. If I had known her true colors, and how things turned out, would I have done things differently? Yes and no. I did what I thought was right at the time and I feel completely confident that where she was concerned I behaved with integrity. What I would do differently is stand up for myself and set some boundaries. I let Brian and his wife intimidate me. I was in a bad place for a long time with my self-esteem, and they both took advantage of that. Unkind of them, to be sure, but I have to own the fact that I allowed it. I also should have had more frank conversations with Brian about the way his wife treated my boys. I avoided those conversations because I knew he would bully me and I would feel bad, but I still should have had them. Ah, the benefits of hindsight are great.

Fortunately for you, my dear readers, I got one of the worst ones. I know many divorced and remarried people, and while there are sometimes differences of opinions, as long as the parties involved are normal human beings, those differences can be worked out.

Other Stories – I didn't think it was right to leave you with only my story because it wasn't very encouraging, so I want to share some others with you.

Cindy divorced her husband, Bob, when their son was just two. They were committed to parenting their son together. She remains close to him even now that their son is in his 30s. They

Scorned, Torn And Reborn

have shared many family meals together, which have included Bob's second wife and her kids, Bob's third wife, Cindy's second husband, and various parents and grandparents and kids and step-kids and grandkids.

Elaine was the stepmom. She and her husband and the kids' mother worked together to raise the kids. They helped each other out to make everyone's lives easier. She and their mother had different strengths and were able to use that acknowledgement to their daughters' advantages. Elaine was the one, with Mom's blessing, who helped her stepdaughter pick out her prom dress. Whenever there were issues with the girls, all three of the parents worked together to resolve them.

Terri and her husband, David, divorced when their sons were in elementary school. During the divorce process, the boys stayed in the house, while Terri and David spent one week at a time there and then somewhere else. David bought his own house and eventually Terri did, as well. Ten years later, they remain friends and continue to parent their children together.

Tom and his wife divorced while their children were very young. Both remarried and had children with their new spouses. All could be seen at their kids' sports events, sitting together with various grandparents, cheering them on.

Jeannette had a daughter with her husband, Dale. They divorced, and Jeannette later had a son with her boyfriend, Brad. Brad is now engaged to a woman who has a son the same age. All three kids can be found on occasion at any of the three households.

The following is an excerpt from a blog post by Lisa Schmidt, blogger and coach:

Rebecca Donovan

"Halloween, other holidays and birthday parties in my family consists of myself and my son, his father, his fiancé and her two daughters, the fiancé's immediate family, her ex and his family, my ex in-laws and my ex-sister-in-law's parents and sister. We were a sight coming down the street—a wall of people and five children. But the absolute best part of Halloween 2015 was when one of the kids pointed to all of us and said to the woman handing out candy, 'Look, here comes my family.' The 3-year-old gets it. Why is it so hard for some adults to fathom such a thing?"

And from an online UK site (Mumsnet.com):

"Only from the perspective of a child... Parents divorced when I was 9 (siblings 7 and 5). Whatever went on for them they never let us know about it. Never said rude things about each other, discussed big parenting issues and backed each other up, didn't get annoyed with us when we did the whole 'I wish I lived with other parent' thing, helped us buy gifts for the other parent, had a routine for contact but were flexible so we didn't have to choose between things like clubs or parties and contact, both came to parents evening/school plays etc., made us feel loved and valued by both of them. Basically they put us first. We're all adults now and with some retrospect I imagine it wasn't always easy for them but they did a fantastic job. They still get on pretty well and are happy to share family occasions and do each other favours. It's something I really appreciate about them both."

Many more stories such as these can be found in the content of books, blogs, and websites. Divorce and remarriage is so commonplace these days that the nuclear family almost seems to be archaic. Whether you think that is progress or a sad state is irrelevant. The family dynamic has changed in the world at large, and it has changed in your world. The best thing we can do for our children and ourselves is to embrace that new dynamic, whether it's just two parents in two separate households, or it includes a host of other ex-spouses, in-laws, and steps.

United Front – It is imperative that you and your ex-husband create a united front to your children. Yes, there are bound to be some variations in parenting styles. One household will have stricter rules while the other one is more relaxed. Usually the mom ends up being the stronger disciplinarian, with dad being all about the fun stuff, but not always. My house was actually more relaxed because I was a single parent, and often out of bandwidth. Dad's house had two adults to keep order, and she was very protective of her orderly cleanliness. As more and more dads are wanting an equal amount of time with the kids, rather than the standard custody rules created by the courts, it's harder to just be the fun parent. As long as dad is still single, he will find himself having to deal with issues he may have taken for granted before. These would be things like homework, cooking dinner, cleaning up after dinner, bedtimes, breakfast, getting the kids to the bus or to school, etc. Your ex-husband may actually develop an appreciation for some of the stuff you did.

To the extent possible, both parents need to be involved in the daily lives of the kids. If soccer practice is on your day, don't be so protective of your specified time that you would discourage their dad if he wants to come. At times it's hard to know what is going to be best for your child in the short term versus the long term. My older son did not always get along with his dad, and especially with his stepmom. There was one time when he called me, very upset, to come get him from his dad's house. My first inclination was to run over there and get him. It was heart-wrenching to listen to him. Instead I took a breath and had a conversation with his dad. Then I talked to my son again and was able to get him calmed down. If he had still wanted me to come get him, I would have (and I told him that), but in the end he made the decision for himself that he could stay the night there. In this case, I deferred my gut reaction to run to the rescue and was instead able to act as a mediator to find a solution. If one of your kids gets in trouble at school, both of you should deal with it. It may seem like you are bonding or doing them a favor, but if you start keeping secrets about your kids from their dad, you open up the possibility of them playing you against each other. Don't let your kids manipulate you this way. You want them to be happy and well adjusted, but they are not the ones who are in charge. That's still you and their dad.

Living Far Apart – As I mentioned before, you can have language in your decree that limits where either spouse can move the children. The restriction in my decree was fine with me because I had no intention of moving them far away from their father. Not everyone feels that way. I knew a guy who was from Germany. He had an ex-wife and son in Germany and married an American woman who lived there. After they had a few kids, she decided to move back to the U.S. He came with her, leaving his oldest child in Germany. His wife then decided to move to another part of the country. He again went with her. The third time she did this, he said enough is enough and she left him with two of the kids and took the other two with her. I know several other men who have followed their ex-wives to another state so they could be with their kids. I know also of women who have agreed to move with the kids to follow dad's new job. I have great admiration and respect for the men and women who would do this, but I also ask them why they didn't get that straight in the decree. I know other men whose ex-wives moved across the country with the kids and they were unable or unwilling to follow. I can't judge why these women chose to make such drastic moves. Certainly, there are unique circumstances that might necessitate a cross-country move, but it should be discussed at length with the father. In my opinion, it is unfair to him and, most especially, to the children, to separate them unless there is some abuse of some sort. I don't mean to pick on women, here, but in most cases, women are the primary guardians, even in 50/50 custody situations, depending on the laws of your state. If you absolutely have to make a big move, it is in everyone's best interest to come to an agreement with your kids' dad to maximize his time with them, even if that means you will have to pay for some plane tickets. I would urge you to engage the services of a family counselor to determine the best course of action. Obviously, if you have primary custody and your ex-husband decides to move away, you have no control over that. In that case, however, it is still important to make what concessions you are able to make so that you do not stand in the way of their continued contact.

This subject is near and dear to my heart. My parents divorced when I was just three. My father had some legal issues, and instead of facing the consequences, he chose to move to another state. He didn't send any child support for two years, and we only saw him once or twice a year after that. To her credit, my mother kept the relationship alive to the extent possible. She told us he loved us, and maybe he did. I once asked Brian what he would choose if he had the choice to spend a few months in jail and then regularly be with his kids or skip jail and only see them a couple of times a year. He didn't hesitate. He said jail. Of

Rebecca Donovan

course. I never got over the rejection of my father's departure, even if he did love me. It affected everything about my life.

You can't control the actions of another person. If dad wants to move, then he'll move, but if there is a way to keep everyone within driving distance, I implore you to examine the possibilities and options.

Remarriage – Statistically, men remarry more often, and sooner, than women. Hopefully the stepparent issue is not concurrent with your divorce. Unfortunately, however, there are a lot of men who leave their wives for another woman, and then turn around and marry that woman as soon as the law allows. And to be fair, there are women who do that, too, although not as often. Unless your children are already grown up and out of the house, your spouse is likely to remarry at some point and create a stepparent for your children. That's when the real fun begins. I have many friends who are and have been stepparents. The cooperative parenting thing really can work, but it obviously depends on the dynamics of ALL the players. Even though my personal experience was a disaster, it doesn't have to be. If things are done in the correct order—divorce, meet someone new, start dating, then get married—there is a much better chance of successful co-parenting. While approximately 50 percent of first marriages end in divorce, the percentage for second marriages is 60 percent, and 70 percent for third. With this in mind, chances are there will be more than one stepmom in your future. Is this getting too depressing? Sorry, just want to reiterate how important it is for you and the father of your children to work out your co-parenting plan as soon as possible and get it in writing to avoid problems down the road.

Scorned, Torn And Reborn

There are challenges ahead. It may seem daunting to parent your children with a person you are no longer married to. When you add the probability of a stepparent on one or both sides, it may be difficult to imagine how it could go smoothly. I have news. Parenting is difficult. It doesn't matter how many or few people are involved in it. It is difficult because you are trying to raise children. Regardless of your parenting styles, children have their own ideas about things and they will create challenges for you that you never knew even existed. That's their job. It is a relief to have someone who loves your children as you do to bounce ideas and concerns off of. While stepparents probably won't feel *exactly* as you do about your kids, they know them and might have some different experience or perspective that will help you. Embrace the changes in your family dynamics. Even with the challenges we faced with my kids' stepmom, it all worked out. Their dad has always been and still is involved in their lives. They grew up. They are good people. At the end of the day, that's all we can really ask for.

Exercises

1. Make a list of five things you and your ex-husband agree on when it comes to parenting.
2. Make a list of five things you disagree about. Order them by importance and discuss the points with him.
3. Make sure your kids know what the schedule is well in advance. It's great if you and their dad are flexible enough to switch things around on occasion, but make sure your kids are in the loop.

Visualization

Sit in a quiet place. Get comfortable. Take a deep breath in through your nose and blow it out very slowly through your mouth. With each breath you let out, imagine a part of your body completely relaxing. Start with your head. When you exhale, feel the tension leaving your head. Next, focus on your neck as you exhale. With each breath, move down your body until you get all the way to your toes. Continue to follow your breath as you imagine you are in a big swimming pool with your kids. Imagine their father is on the other side of them. Put your family—parents and/or siblings—in the pool as well. Form a nice tight circle around your kids. Put dad's family in there, too. Imagine dad has a girlfriend or wife. Put her in the pool. Imagine you have a boyfriend or husband. He goes in there, too. As you all move in a group toward the deep end of the pool, your kids can no longer touch the bottom. That's not a problem because all of the adults surrounding them hold them up. Feel the love everyone in that pool has for your children.

Chapter Fourteen
Let Yourself Shine

> "The foolish man seeks happiness in the distance,
> the wise grows it under his feet."
> — James Oppenheim

We talked about figuring out what you want—what you want to do, where you want to go. Now we need to talk about how you are going to do that. It's one thing to want. It's quite another to do. It's time to spread your wings and not only learn to fly, but actually fly. This flight will not happen all by itself, however. You will have to take some actions to make it happen.

My Story — Writing this book has been very cathartic for me. With every chapter I finalize, I find more areas I can tweak and improve. My story continues to evolve and move forward in a very positive way because I am no longer stuck. My hope for my clients and my readers is that through my experience and insight I can help you move toward where you want and need to be much, much faster than I did.

My biggest issue keeping me stuck was my self-confidence. I was convinced, even if only subconsciously, that I was not going to be able to get a job to support my children and myself. I held this belief even while engaging in a successful business that I built myself. I believed that I wouldn't be able to have a man interested in me. This was also not true. Almost every time I have attended a social event since my divorce, I have had at least one man interested in me. Whether or not that man, or I, was ready at that time to be in a relationship had a definite effect on the outcome of that interest, but the interest was still there. I didn't believe I was a good enough mother. This is another false notion. When Brian was in the process of leaving our marriage, he told me and himself all sorts of things to convince himself that he was justified in making the leap. One of those things was that this new woman, whom he had never once witnessed in interaction with her children, was a better mother than I was. There was a point when I actually wondered if my kids might be better off without me. Without going into what kind of mother she really was, it didn't have anything to do with me. I was a good mother. I have always been a good mother. I let my own insecurity and lack of self-esteem amplify the things he said. I let it define me. It took a long time for me, longer than it should have, but those things do not define me. It has been a struggle to override the doubts and self-sabotage, but I'm doing it. I have taken the advice I offer in this book and I have recreated myself. That recreation is an ongoing, fascinating project. If feels wonderful and empowering to say that only I get to choose who I am and who I can be.

Learn – When I say learn, I mean two separate things. The first is to learn from all the old baggage in the past. The second is to equip ourselves with new knowledge, skills, and talents for the future.

Scorned, Torn And Reborn

Let's talk about the past for a moment. We all have to face the truth about mistakes. We make them—lots of them. We make them in relationships with our parents, our siblings, our friends, our children, our co-workers, and especially with our spouses. If it weren't for mistakes, the world would be a rather dull place. Imagine life without trial and error. There is excitement in taking risks, hoping they end in rewards. Sometime they do. Sometimes they don't. What's imperative is that you made the effort. As I said before, I do not believe that because a marriage ends in divorce it is a mistake or a failure. If you leave it at that and don't apply this experience to "lesson learned," then that is the failure. We must reflect and review. Ask the questions. What happened? Why did it happen? What do I need to do differently next time? Some things are obvious, like next time you are in a committed relationship, don't go out with your friends every night, don't work until 10:00 p.m. every night, don't sleep with the next door neighbor, etc. Most issues arise from more subtle sources, however. When did you or he stop listening, and why? When and why did sex become an obligation? How can you better balance your hobby, work, and kids so that you and your partner of the future can stay connected? By the time it gets to the point of being away more often than not, that is definitely a symptom of a much bigger problem. This is why it's vitally important to take a break after ending an intimate relationship. You must take the time to be honest with yourself so that you can learn from this experience.

Now let's talk about learning for the future. We must commit ourselves to being lifelong learners. Learning doesn't stop when you finish high school or college or even when you get that PhD. As long as we are alive, we should strive to learn. Knowledge is power, and we need to continually soak it up. I love to improve my knowledge. An example is languages. I've been trying to become fluent in Spanish for years. I'm not there yet. I do speak a fair amount of German. I've been to Italy a few times and will brush up nicely on some key Italian words the next time I go. Recently I decided French would be a good idea, so I've begun listening to some CDs in my car. Wherever I go, the least I can do is figure out how to order a glass of wine in the native language. A few years ago, after using QuickBooks accounting software for many years, I decided to really learn how to use it, so I signed up for a class. That class led to my teaching QuickBooks classes for about a year and a half in different cities across the country. It was fun, and I got to mark several states off my travel bucket list. New information in your brain gives you more to think about and more to talk about. It makes you not only more interesting, but more interested as well. And that leads to a thirst for yet more enlightenment.

Growth – Growth goes along with learning. If you try hard enough, it is possible to emerge from a major breakup without experiencing any growth. If you get stuck in the denial stage, or can't get past the blame factor, you could actually remain stagnant. I must assume that if you are reading books such as this one, you are interested in moving forward. The growth you achieve as a result of your experience is the biggest benefit of the entire breakup. It doesn't matter whether you initiated the separation or your partner did. Everyone has not only the opportunity, but the obligation to get something positive out of the whole ordeal. And the most important is personal growth.

There are many different types of personal growth. Emotional growth is extremely important to keep you from repeating some of the damaging behaviors you once engaged in. This does

Scorned, Torn And Reborn

not mean we don't have or show our emotions. It means we understand them better and have more control when it comes to having and showing them, and what actions we subsequently take.

Spiritual growth can be another valuable result of ending a relationship as significant as a marriage. Asking the big questions and reflecting on the answers, whether that is through journaling, meditation, or prayer, will help increase your spiritual awareness.

Physical growth—get into that exercise program, eat healthier food, and get your body in shape. Few people are really where they want to be physically. Even world class athletes are always looking for ways to improve their game. We discussed in earlier chapters the importance of maintaining your health. I had a bone density test done last year for the first time. Like many women my age, I had some bone loss. There was the possibility of pharmaceutical assistance, which I summarily rejected, but also received some sound advice about what I could do for myself. This included lengthening my daily walks, taking calcium, and lifting weights. The level at which I do these three things doesn't get me to a super buff body, but it does make me feel better and helps me maintain a healthy weight. A worthwhile read that addresses this issue (among others) is *Younger Next Year for Women: Live Strong, Fit, and Sexy—Until You're 80 and Beyond*, by Chris Crowley and Henry Lodge, M.D. It's fundamentally about turning back the clock, physically, but it's not just for older women. I first read this book when I was in my mid-forties and still refer back to it. Whatever you choose to read, watch, or do in regard to your physical health, get started today.

Last, but definitely not least, we have intellectual growth. When it becomes necessary to get creative on the money earning front,

Rebecca Donovan

intellectual growth will come in handy. Nothing feeds depression better than dim-witting your mind by sitting in front of the TV like a zombie watching Real Housewives of Zimbabwe. (Actually, that might be interesting.) Have stimulating conversations, read interesting books (trashy novels are great mindless entertainment but don't add much to your mental capacity), and do the crossword puzzle. I read another great book entitled *Keep your Brain Alive* by Lawrence Katz and Manning Rubin. It talks about the physiology of the brain and how mindless routines tend to dull the brain. Changing up routines and learning new things creates new neural pathways to keep the brain active and keep you sharp. These can be simple things, like brushing your teeth left handed, or changing the route you take to work. I gave this book recently to my mother, who was recovering from a minor concussion that had resulted in short term memory loss. She said it was exactly what she needed to help her with that recovery, as well as ongoing memory issues that come with age.

The more we do now to keep ourselves healthy—emotionally, physically, spiritually, and intellectually—the easier it is to maintain good habits as we get older.

Goals – It is imperative that you set goals. Don't just think about them. Write them down. Set daily goals, weekly goals, monthly—you get the picture. When writing down your goals, make sure you can reasonably make them happen. They need to be specific and measurable (finish presentation outline, rather than work on presentation), achievable (lose 10 pounds, rather than look like Kate Moss), realistic (increase income by 10%, rather than make more money than Bill Gates), and time specific (by March 1, rather than sometime this year). In order to move forward, you need to know where you're going. One of my favorite quotes, by Henry Kissinger, is "If you don't know where you're going, all roads lead to nowhere." Goals without action, however, are just New Year's Resolutions. State your goals and then make a plan of action to bring them to fruition. If the goal is realistic and achievable, then you can make it happen. Start small and work your way up. You are probably still in flux at this point, so small, short-term, easily achievable goals will help tone your goal setting muscles. As we go through a life upheaval as substantial as a divorce, our goals will undoubtedly change. That's okay. If the goals you set last year or last month are no longer realistic and achievable, then you need to revisit and reset. The relevant issue with goals is that you are working toward something that will improve your future and bring you to a place of peace and happiness.

Once you've written down your goals, file the paper away and don't think about it again. Those goals will just make themselves happen. **Just kidding!!** I wanted to see if you were paying attention.

Once you have written down your goals, with target dates and action plans, put them where you can see them every day. Each day in your daily planner, to do list, or calendar, list three things you will do that will get you closer to your goals. Make those three things a priority, and then do them.

Faith in You – You must have faith in yourself and faith in the future. The reason I have so much faith in the future is that I know I own my future. I decide what I want, and then I make it happen. I have come to this recently, however. When I first considered what to do as a career after my divorce, (I had a career when I got married, but for a variety of reasons did not want to pursue that) I read some books, which were very helpful, talked to friends, and decided to pursue a career in human resources (HR). I had a considerable amount of experience from owning a company for 10 years with my ex-husband and thought that was a good jumping-off point. I studied diligently and got my professional certification in HR. HR was something I was trying to create as a safety net for myself. It seemed like a stable, respectable professional career with advancement possibilities and decent pay. It then occurred to me, however, that working in HR did not, in fact, actually appeal to me. What I really wanted to do was to write books and do training, coaching, and/or public speaking. So I read quite a few other excellent books and, most importantly for me, engaged the services of a life coach. She has been invaluable in helping me to define who I am and what I want, set goals for what I want to accomplish, attach action plans to those goals, and then provide accountability for me to make them happen. I decided to put faith in myself and invest in my own future. I have had some hiccups and twists and turns along the way, but I am now pursuing the future I see for myself. I don't do this by wishing, planning, or preparing, although planning and preparing are certainly vital first steps. The way I make change in my life is by making my life happen for me instead of letting it happen to me. I am writing and pursuing a career in which I can have a positive impact on people's lives. It always comes back to that for me. The reason it took me so long to get to what I wanted to do was a lack of faith in my abilities and a misguided belief that I couldn't actually have what I really wanted. I thought I had to settle for whatever came my way. That wasn't true for me, and that's not true for you. Remember, however, that as strong as faith is, you still have to take actions before anything will happen. I remember a man in a business networking group who, in answer to the question of how we marketed our businesses, said, "I just pray, and God makes the phone ring." It turned out his business wasn't really where it needed to be. "Faith without works is dead" – James 2:20.

The best thing about being single is that you own your life. You do not have to get someone else to agree before you can plan a vacation. You don't have to get anyone else's permission before you make a large purchase. You want to take a class in Sixteenth century French poetry? There's no one to tell you that you shouldn't do that because it doesn't fall into their interest categories. You want to cut your hair? Do it. You want to do something completely whimsical and frivolous? YOU get to decide how you want to spend your time and your money. Yay!

Exercises

1. Write down three to five goals—things you want to accomplish in the next year. Make sure they are specific, measurable, achievable, realistic, and time sensitive.
2. For each of these goals, write down one thing you will do TODAY to set the goal in motion.
3. Make a list of three to five new things you want to learn. Take action TODAY on at least one of them.

Visualization

Sit in a quiet place. Get comfortable. Take a deep breath in through your nose and blow it out very slowly through your mouth. With each breath you let out, imagine a part of your body completely relaxing. Start with your head. When you exhale, feel the tension leaving your head. Next, focus on your neck as you exhale. With each breath, move down your body until you get all the way to your toes. Continue to follow your breath as you imagine yourself one year from today. What does your perfect day look like? Where are you? Who are you with? What are you doing? Pay attention to every detail. How do you feel? What do you smell? What do you hear? Once you have a clear vision of this day, write about it in your journal or in a notebook. Think about how you are going to make that dream day a reality.

Chapter Fifteen

Dating

I saved this subject for the end of the book because it rightfully should come after all the other subjects in this book are in the works. It is not a good idea to start dating too soon. When is too soon? When is the time right? Experts agree to a time frame somewhere between one and two years after the divorce. It's not entirely clear if that is divorce initiation or divorce finalization. If you look on the internet where ALL the experts are, you'll see a hundred different answers to those questions. So here's the real answer. You start dating when you are ready to start dating. The key is knowing when you are ready. Following are some points to ponder. Are you still grieving the loss of your marriage? If yes, then wait another month or two and ask again. Are you still having problems letting go? If yes, then wait. Do you have trouble containing your anger when talking to him or about him? If yes, then wait. When you go out with friends, do you tend to drink too much? When you stay at home, do you tend to drink too much? Both of these are signals to wait. Do you feel like time is running out and you have to find a man right now? If yes, then absolutely wait.

Take your time to think about what we've discussed in the preceding chapters. Do you feel comfortable in your new home if you have moved? If you are still living in the house you shared with your husband, have you made significant changes to make it your own? Have you made some single friends? Have you really taken the time and effort to figure out what you want and what you don't want? Do you know what your deal breakers are with a new relationship?

Some people don't date for years after the divorce. Some will say they don't want to date until the children are grown. That could possibly be an excuse for something else. I don't recommend waiting that long. It's good to connect with people of the opposite sex, even if it doesn't lead to romance. Once you do think you're ready, start out slowly. Dip your toe in the water before diving in head first.

My Story – I haven't said much about my first marriage. I often refer to it as a "starter marriage." When I got divorced, my mother said it wasn't a real marriage anyway. I'm not entirely sure what she meant. We said our vows in a church. We lived together. We consummated the union. I'm pretty sure it was a real marriage, but I guess she thought that would somehow make me feel better. If it wasn't a real marriage, then maybe it wasn't a real divorce and it didn't hurt so much. I was pretty young when we got married. A lot of my friends from high school were already married, some divorced already. I was running out of time before I became an old maid. I was twenty-one. Perspective can be a devious companion. The marriage itself lasted four years. Although I did love my first husband—we'll call him Jim—we had vastly different ideas about what we wanted in life. It was best to part ways.

Scorned, Torn And Reborn

Because I had been thinking about the parting of ways for about half of the marriage, I felt like I was over it by the time the "I do's" were "I don't-ed." I started dating immediately. And I do mean immediately. I didn't read any books or talk to any professionals, and didn't even know I should do any of those things. I certainly didn't spend any time reflecting on what I wanted or didn't want. I do remember the first morning I woke up after I moved out, I had absolute clarity that I had done the right thing. I felt very free and wasn't about to burden myself with complicated self-reflection. After all, it was all Jim's fault. I hadn't done anything wrong.

I was right about one thing. The divorce was absolutely the right decision. In retrospect, we could have just continued living together instead of getting married. But, and this is a big but, if I had not married Jim, I would most likely have moved back to New Mexico where I was from and then I never would have met Brian, with whom I made a couple of great new people. That's the problem with "if onlys." You get into that whole butterfly effect concept.

The issue with not taking the time for self-reflection is that you are doomed to repeat patterns and keep attracting the same people to you time and time again. My second husband could not have been more different from my first. At least that's the way it seemed on the surface. The problems we faced in our relationship, however, had some striking similarities. When I first started living with Brian, roughly five years after my divorce from Jim, I was constantly struck by Déjà vu. The way he would pick a fight right before he was headed out of town, the way everything was always somehow my fault, my relationship with his mother, etc., were disturbingly familiar. Fortunately for the creation of my children, I chose to ignore all the signs.

Fast forward to divorce number two. I knew I was a mess. I read a lot of books. I talked with a lot of friends, and a few professionals. I did a lot of self-reflection. And I started dating again way too soon. The leader of the divorce class that I took recommended a year. It was absolutely verboten to date anyone from the class while in the class. Of course, people did anyway, and it didn't go well. The first time I ventured out into the dating arena was a few months after my divorce was final. It was with someone from the class. He was still very much in love with his ex-wife, and was probably the most emotionally unavailable man I have ever met, but we had some fun together. There was no hope for that particular relationship to flourish, but I can't say that I really regret it. It was sort of a practice run for both of us. For me, it told me how NOT ready I was for dating. I gave it up for a while after that. Then I met someone six months later that I really liked. We had three great dates, then that one disintegrated into thin air. Couple of dinner dates, a weekend with an old friend, and a blind date thing that went another three dates. All in all—nothing substantial. I decided to concentrate on other things. Then, as many people do, I joined an online dating site. That proved to be unfruitful, but I'll talk more about that below.

If you're hoping this is one of those "see how I met the love of my life in 180 days" books, I'm sorry to disappoint. While I have gone on quite a few dates and had some nice relationships, I've been on a quest to make a better me. When I get to where I need to be, I believe my life partner will show up. And if not, that's okay, too. I'm in a really good place, and I'm still enjoying the ride.

Patterns – We form patterns in our lives from the time we are little children. How is it that some women keep getting involved with abusive men, even though they swear they never will? Why do some men seem to find that wife number two has the same pathological spending habits as number one? Each of my two husbands was unique in so many ways, and yet strikingly similar in the ways that contributed to the downfall of the union. These are the patterns that we get into. That is why it is so vitally important that we take enough time between major relationships to reflect and regroup. It could be that we need to change a few things about what we want, need, and expect from a relationship. We may need to improve on some aspects of ourselves, enter into some personal growth. If we do not allow ourselves to heal completely, we are likely to keep repeating these patterns and attracting mates who are destined to fail us, and we them. I referenced a wonderful book earlier that I found to be immensely helpful in learning to release destructive patterns. *Calling In "The One"* by Katherine Woodward Thomas. While the premise of this book is to help us find "the one," it is so much more than that. It helps the reader to recognize and release the beliefs about oneself that are in the way of being who we really are and who we can be. Once we've done that, and when we are ready to love and be loved, we'll be able to attract the right kind of person.

Online Dating Sites – I know a few people who have met the love of their life through one of these sites, so I would not necessarily discourage their use. Depending on your circumstances, it may be extremely difficult or even impossible to meet people in other ways. If you choose to do this, be careful. There are some good sites and there are some not-so-good sites. Talk to people who have used these sites and get their opinions on which ones are better. Remember that the free, or very cheap, sites appeal to the masses. There are a gazillion people on there,

Rebecca Donovan

and you have to wade through all of them. There are sites that are solely for hooking up, and the players there are, well, players. My recommendation is to choose a site that requires some time, effort, a little bit of money, and a good deal of thought. If someone has to spend a couple of hours answering questions and uploading photos, you know they are taking the whole thing seriously. Otherwise you get people who have invested three minutes uploading a picture (probably an old picture—maybe not even their own), lying about their age, and posting something thought-provoking like "looking for Ms. Right" or "Race Car Driver seeking beautiful navigator." They can be cute and catchy, but what do they really tell you about that person? Maybe their friend even wrote that for them. Many of them are also married and/or just looking for sex. Each site has a disclaimer, usually with advice on taking prudent precautions. Take heed of these precautions. Beware of scammers who ask for money or try to direct you to an alternate site. Don't give personal information at first. I am surprised by the number of people who will post photos of their children, tell where they go to school, etc. Use good judgment and don't jump into this until you are really ready. It can be very time consuming, and you may still need that time for your own healing.

My experience with online dating (over the years I tried several sites) was a mixed bag. I met a few really nice men, but it very rarely led to a second date, as there just wasn't any chemistry happening. Everyone has some amusing stories to tell about online dates. People post photos that were taken many years and many pounds ago. Quite a few people lie about their age and income, and more than a handful of men will lie about their height. I guess they think you will be so enamored by their charming personality and witty conversation that you won't notice those things. On the contrary, I found most of my online dates to be lacking in the charm and conversation department. They would drone on and on about themselves, and I couldn't get a word in edgewise. Many of them had leftover hostility about their ex-wives. You can learn an awful lot about someone by the way they talk about their ex-spouse. Remember that when you talk about yours, which you shouldn't even do until asked.

If you decide to give it a try, here are some tips. Post pictures of yourself that are current within a couple of years. Include a close-up and some pictures that show you doing things you enjoy. Don't include a bunch of pictures of your pets. Don't include pictures of your children. Don't post pictures of you standing next to someone who is way more attractive than you. Don't post overly sexy pictures or drunken party pics. Make your profile short and sweet—and honest. Nobody wants to read a novel. Don't waste a lot of time emailing. Two to four emails is enough to determine if you want to meet someone. Don't give your last name or your phone number right away. (Google your first name and phone number and see what comes up.) ALWAYS meet in a public place. Choose something that has a limited timeframe, like coffee or lunch. If he does not offer to pick up the bill, don't make a second date. Try to relax and just be yourself. If you are nervous, it's okay. He is probably nervous, too. Think of it as practice. You have all the time in the world.

Dating for the Ages – 20s, 30s, 40s, and Beyond – The first time I got divorced, I was only 26 years old. Dating at that point wasn't significantly different from what I had done before. There were a lot of people out there who were single, some divorced, but from relatively short marriages, and

Rebecca Donovan

not that many with kids. Fast forward to my late 40s after an 18-year relationship and everything (almost) had changed about dating. People have had time to have a couple of marriages, kids, maybe even grandkids. There is more baggage hanging around single people at this stage than there is at Chicago O'Hare Airport. Everywhere you look, people are lonely, but also afraid to get out there and muck it up again. They find it difficult to trust anyone, least of all themselves and their own judgement. These are the casualties of relationships gone bad, exacerbated by nasty, undignified divorces. It doesn't have to be that way. You definitely don't have to be that way.

If you've been off the market, so to speak, for a number of years, you will find dating to be quite different. There's much more texting and much less dialing. The demographics in your geographic region will dictate the dating climate. I was single for a long time in Austin, TX. It is a young city with more women than men, so that creates a bit more of a challenge for women over 40. I read some interesting books on dating, but they were mostly superficial and written for younger people. It is imperative to have a sense of humor—and patience. As I said before, you have time to ease back into it. You don't have to rush anything, so the best thing you can do is take a few deep breaths and relax. And keep your expectations at a reasonable level. My experience with many people, men in particular, who have been married for a long time is that they immediately want to feel that level of comfort that they had with their spouse. They don't realize that it just isn't going to happen in a few dates. Even when your marriage wasn't going well, there was still this comfort zone that you miss when you are on your own. Perhaps that's why so many people jump far too quickly into second (or third) marriages. They want to get back to that comfort zone without having to take the time

182

to build the necessary infrastructure. They want the "Advance to Marvin Gardens" card without having to roll the dice. Slow down. Take your time. Reflect on your strengths and weaknesses so that you can work on your own issues and recognize issues you want to steer clear of in others. Learn to be excited again at the prospect of starting something new. Go in with your eyes and your heart open, but pace yourself and build the foundation before you try to put in a cozy den.

Bars – Once you realize you have the freedom to do whatever you want, you may find yourself going to bars a lot. This can be a good source of letting loose and having fun. Some people meet the great loves of their lives in bars. I actually met both of my husbands in bars. The first we both worked in, and the second was in the taco line at happy hour. However, being in bars can get old pretty fast for several reasons. For one thing, people you meet there are often intoxicated. You, yourself, may be intoxicated, which, as you may know, can lead to some questionable judgment calls. Going home from a bar with someone you just met may seem like the thing to do at the time, but truly almost never makes you feel good in the long run. Things have changed in the past twenty (or more) years, and to avoid unwanted diseases and normal-seeming people who are, in reality, psychotic freaks, keep your wits about you (i.e., moderate your drinking) while in bars, especially if you are there by yourself. In addition, there is that driving home while under the influence thing. Be smart about this (i.e., call a taxi or Uber), especially if you are drinking more than you are used to.

All that being said, there is nothing wrong with going to a bar by yourself, especially if you are there for something besides just the alcohol. Sports bars are great places to watch your favorite sporting events. It beats sitting at home alone to watch because it's always more fun to cheer with other people, and it's an easy conversation starter. When you want to take yourself out for dinner, sit at the bar if there is one. You generally get seated faster, the service is often better, and you have the added bonus of chatting with your fellow solo diners. If you are interested in conversation with other humans, leave the phone in your pocket or purse. If you do want to be left alone, nothing says that quite like earbuds. Also, if you really want to be ALONE, then sit at a table instead and save the bar stools for people who want to connect.

A word of caution about going to bars by yourself: if you are feeling desperate, sitting alone at a bar is the worst place to be. It will not make you feel better. Desperation is unattractive at best and leads to others taking advantage of you at worst. There will be times when you feel lonely. That's normal. I can't stress this enough: you have time. There is no rush. There is no contest that you have to win. You are worth the time it takes to get where you need to be.

Other Ways to Meet Potential Dates – When you do something you enjoy with other people who enjoy that same thing, there is good potential to meet someone with whom you share an interest. I will again mention Meetup groups. If you want to meet men, steer toward things men like to do. Think beer, outdoor activities, cars, and sports. If you live in an area where country and western dancing is popular, willing dance partners can be found there. They are usually pretty polite, too. If the Meetup is to go see a romantic comedy, that is probably just a girls' night kind of thing. A Meetup to watch the football playoffs? Men. Local brew pubs or a beer tasting adventure?

Men. Many areas will host some kind of speed dating. I haven't tried that, but I've heard it can be fun. Dog parks have a pretty even mixture of people. If your well-meaning married friends want to set you up on a date, consider doing it. Yes, blind dates can be awful—everyone has a story—but they can also be fun. It is the way a lot of people have gotten together. Be open. Relax. Have fun.

Sex – For many people, when the marriage is not going well, the frequency of sex will diminish. I've met people who say it had been years since they had sex with their spouse. In general, sex is a healthy part of the marriage package. If it has really been years (I find that men sometimes exaggerate in this area), then nobody should be surprised about the breakup—only why it took so long.

Once you are divorced, and can do whatever you want to do, you will probably want to have some sex. Maybe a lot of sex. You are, after all, making up for lost time, right? There's nothing wrong with that as long as you are: A) not having it with your ex, B) not doing something that will damage your self-respect, and C) being honest with the person with whom you are having sex. Sometimes sex can be just sex. Both parties need to be in agreement on that point. If you have been in a long-term relationship, the thought of having sex with someone else can be daunting. It's not like when we were in our 20s. As we get older, spontaneity is just not what it used to be. Trust is a bigger factor now. Getting drunk and picking up strangers in a bar is really not the way to go, generally speaking. You guys saw *Fatal Attraction*, right? Again, do what makes you feel good about yourself. Don't let your friends or some ridiculously unrealistic movie influence you on this point. Follow your instincts. Oh, yeah, and use a condom!

Rebecca Donovan

If Something Seems Like It's Too Good To Be True...

When I first got divorced, the term "cougar" was annoyingly popular. I am not fond of stereotypes, labels, or titles, especially ones that are unfairly applied. So it is with the title of cougar. Although very few people can tell what the origin of this term is, I believe it originally referred to a divorced woman of a certain age (over 40? Over 50?) skanking about, looking for much younger men to seduce. The term seems to have morphed into a description of any woman over 30 who is out in a public place, such as a bar or restaurant, unescorted by a man. It is a condescending remark made mostly by those who are married or in a relationship and smugly think they are somehow superior because of it. It is these sanctimonious individuals who are the most surprised when they find themselves single again. As the rug can be yanked out from under us at any time without warning, we should all be a little less judgmental of others, lest we someday walk in their shoes. A little bit of an age difference shouldn't be a big deal. If you happen to meet someone interesting who is not your exact age, who cares? It isn't anyone else's business. I personally prefer to date men who are within 10 years of my age either way. There are, however, some situations that cross over into creepiness—at least for me. I was out with a girlfriend recently and was talking to a couple of young soldiers at the bar. As a gesture of appreciation for their service to our country, I bought them a drink. One of them (24) told me I was hot, and asked me for my phone number. I was taken aback, but moderately flattered. It became immediately obvious, however, that he was looking for a sugar mama to take care of him while he went to school. Ego boost to ego bust in nothin' flat. As the voice of reason will tell you, there are limits, so regardless of how good you THINK you look, do be cautious.

Scorned, Torn And Reborn

When something appears too good to be true (like when you are 50+ and 30 pounds overweight and they are in their 20s and *super hot*), guess what? It probably is. (Yes, I'm aware that there are exceptions and try to shy away from absolutes, but in my experience...) If you have the good fortune to have a good fortune, don't advertise that fact to impress the youngsters. It never feels good to be used, and at this point in your life you don't need the extra aggravation.

When you start dating again, do have some discretion. If you still have children at home, be selective about who you bring around the house. Talk to your kids about your decision to start dating. They may be perfectly fine with it, even encourage you, but if they are secretly hoping you and dad will get back together, you may face some resistance. If dad is already dating, that will pave the way for you. If dad is not already dating, or if your kids don't realize that he is, perhaps you and he can have a conversation with the kids together, so they don't get the idea that one of you is somehow betraying the other. Once you have started to date again, if you start to see too many uncomfortable similarities to your ex-husband and find yourself headed down an old familiar path, take a pause. Go back and revisit what you really want and what you really don't want.

Exercises

1. Make a list of five things you absolutely must have in a potential partner.
2. Make a list of five things you absolutely do not want in a potential partner.
3. Ask a girlfriend to go on a "practice date" with you. Get her feedback on how you present yourself.

Visualization

Sit in a quiet place. Get comfortable. Take a deep breath in through your nose and blow it out very slowly through your mouth. With each breath you let out, imagine a part of your body completely relaxing. Start with your head. When you exhale, feel the tension leaving your head. Next, focus on your neck as you exhale. With each breath, move down your body until you get all the way to your toes. Continue to follow your breath as you imagine you are on the perfect date. Where do you go? What does your date look like? What does he talk about? Imagine him listening to you with interest and laughing easily when you say something witty. You feel completely safe and comfortable. Pay attention to the circumstances that allow you to feel this way.

Chapter Sixteen

Reborn

> "We must be willing to get rid of the life we've planned, so as to have the life that is waiting for us. The old skin has to be shed before the new one can come.
> — Joseph Campbell

Recovering from a divorce is an ongoing process. You will do it at your own pace, depending on what feels right for you. Many factors come into play along the way that will propel you forward, and just as many will become cumbersome roadblocks. Getting past these blocks may be something you can do alone, with the help of friends and family, or it may require some professional help in the form of a therapist or coach. If you are stumbling along the way, don't get discouraged. If you are coming from a place of integrity and honesty, you will prevail and become the person you always wanted to be. Do not be afraid or embarrassed if you need some help. We all need help. It is not a sign of weakness to seek assistance. Rather it is a sign of strength that you are willing to do what you need to do to move forward.

Quest – You are on a quest—an adventure. This is your time to explore, to discover, and to chart new territories. It's your chance to start over and be whoever you want to be. You have only the limits you impose on yourself. There is no one to tell you that you're not good enough, strong enough, or smart enough. You no longer have to dream someone else's dream, work for someone else's goal, or do someone else's laundry. You are absolutely free to become who you were always meant to be. Embark on this journey of self-discovery. You will be amazed at what you find along the way.

Value – Before anyone else can value us, we have to value ourselves. This comes into play in all aspects of our lives, not just in relationships. We draw to ourselves a reflection of how we feel about ourselves. If you are doing a job where you are not getting the promotion you seek, or the raise you expected, or the recognition you wanted, think about how you truly value yourself in that position. I was doing a job gratis for a while to help a start-up company. The work, while essential, was clerical in nature, and not very interesting to me. I did what was necessary for the most part, but it lingered on much longer than anticipated, and I began to resent doing it for free. When I asked for (demanded, really) some pay and got it, then I just felt obligated. I had to step back and realize that I resented not being valued by the company because I wasn't valuing myself in doing that work. I stopped doing it, and it felt great. The same is true in a relationship—any relationship. How do you value yourself in the relationship? If you believe you are inferior in some way, others will view you that way as well and treat you accordingly.

Gifts – You have been given many gifts. I touched on this previously when encouraging you to acknowledge the gifts your partner gave you that cannot be taken away. Think now about all of the other gifts you have. This is crucial to the whole healing process, particularly healing with dignity. I now believe that when my former husband left me he gave me a gift. It was as though I had been given back myself. I am now free to be exactly who I am and who I want to be. I am no longer constrained by someone else's expectations. If you look at a hardship as a gift, it can actually become one. Many things in our lives seem difficult, but that is by design to help us grow. One of my sons gave me a hard time on things like homework, and chores, and discipline, and just about everything else as he tested his boundaries. All of these things, while incredibly irritating and frustrating at times, have helped me immeasurably in my personal journey. Take adversity, take unfairness, and take your pain. Make them work for you in new and creative ways. Nobody said it would be easy. Envision yourself on the other side of the difficulty.

Giving – Enough about the gifts we have received. I read an article recently by a woman with multiple sclerosis who received some strange but sound advice from a friend in response to her complaints about her illness. No one can question the debilitating nature of this illness or this woman's right to complain about it, but it turned out she could actually do something to make herself feel better. Complaining, as far as I know, does not achieve that positive result. Her friend told her to give 29 gifts in 29 days. At first she thought that was dumb but eventually came back to it and tried it. Obviously it did not cure her disease, but it helped immensely in the way she looked at it and at herself. I tried this, and it felt pretty good. I might not have made the whole 29 days, but something is definitely better than nothing. Give. Give your time. Give someone a physical gift (it does not have to be expensive). Give positive energy. Listen to someone who needs an ear. Give a hug, a smile, an encouraging word. No matter how bad you may be feeling, lifting someone else's spirits cannot help but lift yours as well.

Happiness – At the beginning of this breakup, happiness probably seems like a far-away dream. I know that's how I felt at first. I wondered if I would ever be happy again. The reality is YES—yay!—you will be happy again. When you are ready to let go of all the emotions and attachments that are keeping you down and embrace your new life with enthusiasm, you will feel happiness again. The happiness you feel being on your own is a bit different from the happiness of being with someone you love. One is not better than the other, except the stress factor goes down when you are not trying to keep someone else happy. You gain contentment from the inner strength you may be surprised to find you have in such abundance. You do not need someone else to make you happy. You can certainly BE happy with another person, but that person doesn't make you happy. You do that for yourself. My hairdresser, Michael (he's awesome), offered this observation: "I have never met a woman who wasn't happier after her divorce than she was when she was married. It usually takes about a year, but then she is lighter, laughs more, and in general is much better off."

Wherever you are in the divorce process, whether you've just received the news, or if you're already on the other side of the split, know that I've been there and I understand. Moreover, there are thousands of your sisters out there who also understand. If you are not able to connect with any of them in person through local resources, at least find them in cyberspace, through a virtual retreat, Facebook group, or relevant blogs. Remember, this is not a race. You are worth the time and effort it takes to get to where you need to be. Everyone must go at their own pace. You may see women who just got divorced and they seem to have it all together, taking it in stride. Meanwhile, you consider it a major accomplishment just to get out of bed every day. First of all, those women just may be hanging on by a thread, and the stress of being a good faker is just about to do them in. Don't assume anything, and maybe reach out to them. You may be exactly what they need and vice versa. I would have loved to have more people reach out to me when I was in the middle of my tormented distress. With so many resources available to you, many of them free, and so many other women in your position, *you do not have to go through this alone.* No man is an island— and no woman is either. Let people help you.

Regardless of your station in life, getting a divorce is nothing to be ashamed of. No one has a right to judge you, and you need not be embarrassed about the whole thing. Hold your head high, and you will come out ahead. This is truly your opportunity to become the person you always wanted to be. Take this experience as the learning tool that it is. You can now do what you want to do. Go where you want to go. Be who you want to be. You are REBORN.

Resources

Books

A New Earth by Eckhart Tolle

Calling In "The One" by Katherine Woodward Thomas

Conscious Uncoupling by Katherine Woodward Thomas

Feelings Buried Alive Never Die by Karol K. Truman

Keep your Brain Alive by Lawrence Katz and Manning Rubin

On Death and Dying by Elisabeth Kübler-Ross

The Desire Map by Danielle LaPorte

The Mastery of Love by Don Miguel Ruiz

The Spiritual Divorce by Debbie Ford

When Your Relationship Ends by Bruce Fisher

Younger Next Year for Women: Live Strong, Fit, and Sexy—Until You're 80 and Beyond, by Chris Crowley and Henry Lodge, M.D.

Websites

www.afsTravelers.com

www.Meetup.com

www.Wevorce.com

CPSIA information can be obtained
at www.ICGtesting.com
Printed in the USA
LVHW04s0740031018
592201LV00003B/3/P